WARRIOR • 166

# ROMAN LEGIONARY AD 69–161

**ROSS COWAN**                    ILLUSTRATED BY SEÁN Ó'BRÓGÁIN

*Series editor Marcus Cowper*

First published in 2013 by Osprey Publishing
PO Box 883, Oxford, OX1 9PL, UK
PO Box 3985, New York, NY 10185-3985, USA
Email: info@ospreypublishing.com

Osprey Publishing is part of the Osprey Group.

A CIP catalogue record for this book is available from the British Library.

Print ISBN: 978 1 78096 587 1
PDF e-book ISBN: 978 1 4728 0283 5
EPUB e-book ISBN: 978 1 4728 0284 2

Editorial by Ilios Publishing Ltd, Oxford, UK (www.iliospublishing.com)
Index by Sandra Shotter
Typeset in Sabon and Myriad Pro
Originated by PDQ Media, UK
Printed in China through World Print Ltd.

13 14 15 16 17   11 10 9 8 7 6 5 4 3 2

www.ospreypublishing.com

## ACKNOWLEDGEMENTS

The author would like to thank all those who made photographs available. Special thanks to the Cowan family, Dr Duncan B. Campbell, Marcus Cowper, Dr Florian Himmler, Thomas McGrory, Steven D. P. Richardson, Seán Ó'Brógáin and Graham Sumner. Quotations from ancient literary sources have been adapted from the Loeb Classical Library.

## ARTIST'S NOTE

Readers may care to note that the original paintings from which the colour plates in this book were prepared are available for private sale. All reproduction copyright whatsoever is retained by the Publishers. All enquiries should be addressed to:

Seán Ó'Brógáin Srath an Ghallaigh, An Clochan, Leifear, Tir Chonaill, Ireland

The Publishers regret that they can enter into no correspondence upon this matter.

## THE WOODLAND TRUST

Osprey Publishing are supporting the Woodland Trust, the UK's leading woodland conservation charity, by funding the dedication of trees.

# CONTENTS

# ROMAN LEGIONARY AD 69–161

## INTRODUCTION

From the great battles at Cremona to the disaster at Elegeia, the period AD 69–161 was filled with drama for the Roman legions. At least three legions were destroyed in battle, two more mysteriously vanished, and others were reconstituted or disbanded for rebellion. New legions were created for wars of conquest in Germany and Dacia, and participated in the great, but ephemeral, expansion of the Roman Empire to the head of the Persian Gulf.

In this book, we will examine the life of the typical Roman legionary of AD 69–161, in some cases from his birth in camp. We will investigate how old he was at enlistment and, once a regular, his rates of pay and prospects of promotion. We will examine how his legion was organized for battle, how he was trained for combat, and what his life was like on campaign. The legionary's experience of battle, the rewards he might win for valiant acts, and his rituals of celebration are considered. We will encounter recruits barely into their teens, grizzled centurions with more than 50 years of service, and training instructors who put their methods into practice on the battlefield.

This was an age in which the legions ceased to be Italian. Provincial recruits almost entirely replaced Italians, but within the confines of the camp and the distinct society of the military, the Roman-ness of the legionaries remained incredibly strong.

**LEFT**
Domitian (AD 81–96). An important figure in the history of the legions, he raised military pay, prohibited the brigading of two legions in one camp, and founded *legio I Flavia Minervia*. (© D. Entwistle)

**RIGHT**
Trajan (AD 98–117), one of the last great Roman conquerors. He created two legions, *II Traiana* and *XXX Ulpia*. (© seriykotik1970)

# CHRONOLOGY

(**All dates** AD)

| | |
|---|---|
| 68 | Rebellions of Vindex, Galba and Macer. Suicide of Nero (June); Galba proclaimed emperor. Formation of legions *I Adiutrix* and *VII Hispana* (later *Gemina*). |
| 69 | Praetorians murder Galba and elevate Otho (January). German legions proclaim Vitellius emperor; Vitellian legions invade Italy and defeat Otho at Cremona; suicide of Otho (April). Revolt of Civilis in the Rhineland. Flavius Vespasian (conducting war against rebels in Judaea) is hailed emperor by his legions. Flavian legions under Antonius Primus invade Italy, defeat Vitellians at second battle of Cremona (October); capture of Rome and death of Vitellius (December). |
| 70 | Civilis' revolt spreads; establishment of Gallic Empire and destruction of *legio XV Primigenia*. Petillius Cerialis defeats Civilis and restores order. Titus, son of Vespasian, destroys Jerusalem. *II Adiutrix* recognized as *iusta legio*. 'New' legions *IV* and *XVI Flavia*. |
| 74 | Capture of Masada; Jewish War ends. |
| 79 | Death of Vespasian; Titus becomes emperor. |
| 81 | Death of Titus; succeeded by his younger brother, Domitian. |
| 82–84 | Caledonians attack *legio VIII Hispana*. Creation of *legio I Minervia*; Domitian conquers Chatti. Agricola defeats Caledonians at Mons Graupius. Domitian increases military pay. |
| 85–88 | War with Dacians; two major Roman defeats followed by victory at Tapae. |
| 89 | Revolt of Antonius Saturninus supported by legions *XIV Gemina* and *XXI Rapax*. Domitian bans practice of two legions sharing a single fortress. |
| 92 | Domitian's war against Sarmatians and Suebi; Sarmatians destroy a legion, perhaps *XXI Rapax*. |
| 96 | Domitian assassinated; senator Nerva made emperor. |
| 97 | Trajan defeats Germans. |
| 98 | Death of Nerva; Trajan succeeds. |
| 101–102 | Trajan's First Dacian War. Establishment of legions *II Traiana* and *XXX Ulpia*. |

The emperor Hadrian (AD 117–138). A former legionary tribune and commander, he ensured the legions were highly trained and always ready for war. (© Marie-Lan Nguyen)

| 105–106 | Trajan's Second Dacian War; defeat and suicide of Decebalus; Dacia added to Roman Empire. Annexation of Nabataean kingdom. |
|---|---|
| 113–116 | Trajan's Parthian War; conquest of Armenia, Assyria and Mesopotamia. Rebellion of conquered regions coincides with revolt of Jewish Diaspora. |
| 117 | Death of Trajan; accession of Hadrian. |
| 118 | Trajan's eastern conquests, except Armenia, relinquished. |
| 122 | Hadrian in Britain; construction of Hadrian's Wall begins. Apis riots in Alexandria; destruction of *legio XXII Deiotariana*? Revolt in Mauretania. |
| 130 | Hadrian founds colony of Aelia Capitolina at Jerusalem. |
| 132–135 | Bar Kochba revolt in Judaea; destruction of *XXII Deiotariania*? |
| 135 | Alani threaten Cappadocia; repulsed by Arrian. |
| 138 | Death of Hadrian; Antoninus Pius succeeds. |
| 139–142 | Reconquest of southern and central Scotland; construction of Antonine Wall. |
| 152 | Suppression of Moorish revolt. |
| 157–158 | Fighting in Dacia. |
| 161 | Death of Antoninus Pius; succession of Marcus Aurelius. Destruction of a legion (*VIIII Hispana*?) at Elegeia. |

# THE FORMATION AND DESTRUCTION OF LEGIONS

Nero raised *legio I Italica* in AD 66 or 67 for a planned campaign in the Caucasus (Suetonius, *Nero* 19.2). Soon after, in preparation for the looming civil war, the emperor formed what was to become *legio I Adiutrix* from drafts of marines from the Imperial Fleet at Misenum. This ad hoc formation was brutally repressed by Galba, but he subsequently recognized it as a *iusta legio*, a regular legion (Tacitus, *Histories* 1.6, 36; Suetonius, *Galba* 12.2; Dio 55.24.12, 64.3.1–2).

When he launched his rebellion in AD 68, Galba reinforced the sole legion in his Spanish army (*VI Victrix*) by enrolling *legio VII Hispana* (Dio 55.24.3; Tacitus, *Histories* 2.11, 3.22; *AE* 1972, 203 for the title). It is better known as *VII Galbiana* (Tacitus, *Histories* 2.86), but was soon re-titled *Gemina*, 'Twin', suggesting that it was merged with another legion, probably because of the heavy casualties it suffered at the second battle of Cremona in AD 69 (cf. Tacitus, *Histories* 3.22).

Another legion was formed in AD 68. The short-lived *legio I Macriana* was named after its founder, Clodius Macer, the rebellious governor of Africa. Galba had Macer murdered and disbanded the legion. It was subsequently reconstituted by Vitellius but we know nothing of its activities (Tacitus, *Histories* 1.11, 2.97). It was presumably disbanded again following the defeat of Vitellius.

*Legio II Adiutrix* was recognized by Vespasian as a *iusta legio* in AD 70 (*ILS* 1989; Dio 55.24.3 for Vespasian as its founder). Like *I Adiutrix*, it drew its original complement from the navy, and is perhaps to be connected with the volunteers from the Ravenna fleet who 'demanded service with the legions', or the ad hoc legion of Vitellian marines that defected to the Flavians at Narnia (Tacitus, *Histories* 3.50, 55, 63).

The two other new legions of Vespasian's reign, *IV Flavia Felix* and *XVI Flavia Firma*, appear to have been reconstitutions of *IV Macedonica* and *XVI Gallica*, compromised by their adherence to Vitellius and involvement in the revolt of Civilis. *Legio I Germanica* also disappears from the army lists. Again, its Vitellian sympathies and collaboration with Civilis (Tacitus, *Histories* 4.12–37, 54ff.) probably resulted in its disbandment, but some of its personnel may have been enrolled into Galba's *legio VII*, hence the new title of 'Twin' (Birley 1928). It is possible that it also received the remnant of *legio XV Primigenia* (the survivors of the detachment that fought for Vitellius in Italy), but the main body of the legion was destroyed in AD 70.

After enduring a long siege in the fortress they shared at Vetera (modern Xanten in Germany), the starving and desperate *legio XV Primigenia*, and remainder of *V Alaudae* (the bulk of the legion was in Italy), surrendered to Civilis in AD 70. As the legionaries marched from their fortress, they were betrayed:

Petilius Secundus of *legio XV Primigenia*. Formed in AD 39, the legion was destroyed 31 years later at Vetera. *ILS* 2275. (© AD Meskins)

Loyalty on the one hand, famine on the other, kept the besieged hesitating between honour and disgrace. As they thus wavered, their sources of food, both usual and even unusual, failed them, for they had consumed their beasts of burden, their horses, and all other animals, which, even though unclean and disgusting, necessity forced them to use. Finally, they tore up even shrubs and roots and grasses growing in the crevices of the rocks, giving thereby a proof at once of their miseries and of their endurance, until at last they shamefully stained what might have been a splendid reputation by sending a delegation to Civilis and begging for their lives. He refused to hear their appeals until they swore allegiance to the Empire of Gaul. He then stipulated for the booty of their camp and sent guards to secure the treasure, the camp followers, and the baggage, and to escort the soldiers as they left their camp empty-handed. When they had proceeded about five miles the German troops suddenly attacked and beset them as they advanced unsuspicious of any danger. The bravest were cut down where they stood, many were slain as they scattered; the rest escaped back to camp. Civilis, it is true, complained of the Germans' action and reproached them for breaking faith shamefully. But whether this was mere pretence on his part, or whether he was unable to hold their fury in check is not certainly proved. His troops plundered the camp and set it on fire; the flames consumed all who had survived the battle.

Tacitus, *Histories* 4.60

Iulius Maternus, a veteran of *legio I Minervia*. The legion was created by Domitian to fight in the Chattan war of AD 83. *CIL* XIII 8267a. (© Hannibal21)

It is unclear why *legio V Alaudae* fades from the army lists at this time. Fighting in Italy (impressively forcing *XIII Gemina* from the field at the first battle of Cremona), and with its small remainder besieged in Vetera, it was not involved in the collaboration with Civilis that so tainted other German legions. It may be that the legion suffered massive casualties at the second battle of Cremona (Tacitus, *Histories* 2.43 and 3.22).

A sole inscription has been taken to suggest that *V Alaudae* did survive the upheavals of AD 69–70 and was transferred to a new base in Moesia (*IMS* VI 41). The inscription actually commemorates a veteran of *V Alaudae* in a colony at Scupi. A new base for the legion elsewhere in Moesia has been inferred from this (and Tacitus' remark about defeated Vitellians being sent to Illyricum: *Histories* 3.35), but the colony, which included veterans from other Vitellian legions, may have been a gesture of reconciliation by Vespasian and need not imply that *legio V Alaudae* also relocated to the Balkans. The end of the legion has been linked with the catastrophic defeat of Cornelius Fuscus by the Dacians in AD 86. Dio implies that a legionary eagle standard was lost in this battle (68.9.3 – its recovery by Trajan), but the loss of an eagle need not equate to the destruction of a legion. The fate of *V Alaudae* remains unresolved.

At least one legion was destroyed during the reign of Domitian, and another was created. The emperor created *legio I Flavia Minervia* (Dio 55.24.3), probably in connection with his war against the Chatti and conquest of the Agri Decumates in AD 82/3 (*ILS* 2279 gives original titles – *Flavia* was subsequently dropped – and suggests formation no later than AD 83). Domitian's military fortunes were mixed, and in AD 92 the Sarmatians destroyed one of his legions (Suetonius, *Domitian* 6.1; Eutropius, *Breviarium* 7.23).

The most likely candidate is *XXI Rapax*. In AD 89, along with *legio XIV Gemina*, with which it shared a fortress at Mogontiacum (Mainz), it supported the revolt of Antonius Saturninus, the governor of Upper Germany. Saturninus and his forces, presumably including the two legions, were defeated in battle. Domitian then banned the practice of brigading two legions in the same camp (cf. Suetonius, *Domitian* 6.2, 7.3). The disgraced *XXI Rapax* was consequently sent to another fortress. In AD 92/3, *legio XXII Primigenia* occupied Mogontiacum; *XIV Gemina* had been transferred to Pannonia, perhaps to fill a gap left by the annihilation of *XXI Rapax*.

The emperor Trajan raised two legions, *II Traiana Fortis* and *XXX Ulpia Victrix* (Dio 55.24.3–4), for service in his Dacian Wars (AD 101–102 and 105–106). Another 50 years would pass before an emperor enrolled new legions (*II* and *III Italica* by Marcus Aurelius in AD 165, belatedly replacing legions destroyed in the intervening period).

The last mention of *legio XXII Deiotariana* is in a letter written by the emperor Hadrian in AD 119. The emperor advises the *praefectus* (equestrian governor) of Egypt on the rights of the sons of legionaries of *XXII Deiotariana*, and its sister unit *III Cyrenaica*, to inherit the property of their fathers (*BGU* I 140). Serving soldiers (probably including centurions) were not allowed to contract legal marriages until the end of the 2nd century AD, and any children born before *honesta missio* (honourable discharge) was granted were

Duccius Rufinus, standard-bearer of *legio VIIII Hispana*. The Ninth Legion may have been destroyed at the battle of Elegeia in AD 161. *RIB* I 673. (© RHC Archive)

9

considered illegitimate. The unit is not included in the famous list of the legions inscribed on two columns in Rome (*ILS* 2288, probably dating to the reign of Antoninus Pius, or perhaps the start of the reign of Marcus Aurelius). Some suppose it met its end in Judaea during the Bar Kochba rebellion (AD 132–135); Dio implies heavy legionary casualties (69.13.1). Another possibility is the Alexandrian riots of AD 121/122, which were triggered by disputes between the native Egyptians over the appearance of the sacred bull, Apis (Historia Augusta, *Hadrian* 12.1).

The disappearance of the Ninth Legion continues to fascinate. *Legio VIIII Hispana* did have a brush with disaster in AD 82, when the Caledonians broke into its camp (Tacitus, *Agricola* 26), but only fantasists and nationalists, clinging to the factoid deriving from Rosemary Sutcliff's *The Eagle of the Ninth*, continue to assert that the legion was destroyed in Scotland in *c.* AD 117. The legion certainly existed after this date. Lucius Aemilius Karus' tribunate in the legion cannot be dated before AD 122 (*ILS* 1077), and Numisius Iunior is unlikely to have served as *tribunus laticlavius* (senatorial tribune) before AD 140 (*CIL* XI 5670).

The Ninth Legion left Britain early in the 2nd century AD; it is last recorded at its camp in York in AD 108 (*RIB* 665). It was based for a time at Nijmegen and may have been sent east to quell the Bar Kochba revolt (AD 132–135). An epitaph from Naples could suggest that the Ninth was brought up to full fighting strength by a transfer of marines from the fleet at Misenum (*CIL* X 1769). Like *XXII Deiotariana*, the legion is missing from the column lists in Rome (*ILS* 2288). Something catastrophic occurred to the legion between AD 140 (the tribunate of Numisius Iunior) and 161 (the accession of Marcus Aurelius and the latest date for the inscribing of the column lists in their original form). The battle of Elegeia in AD 161 may offer a solution to the mystery.

As the Judaean rebellion was drawing to a close in AD 135, Cappadocia (eastern Turkey) came under pressure from the Alani, an Iranian people renowned for their cavalry (Dio 69.15.1). Flavius Arrian, the governor of Cappadocia, succeeded in repulsing the Alani with the legions *XII Fulminata* and *XV Apollinaris* and a substantial force of auxiliaries, but to guard against future incursions, it may have been considered prudent to add another legion to the garrison of the vulnerable province. The Ninth Legion, assuming it had been sent east to fight the Jews, could have provided a major reinforcement to the Cappadocian garrison. However, it should be noted that the governors of Cappadocia were not of a seniority to be entrusted with three legions; emperors were always wary of giving ambitious men too many soldiers.

The Parthians invaded Armenia in AD 161. Sedatius Severianus, governor of neighbouring Cappadocia, moved to expel them, but his army, apparently composed of a little more than a single legion, was surrounded at Elegeia. With their massive superiority in archers, the Parthians pinned the Romans down for three days. Severianus despaired and committed suicide, as did his chief centurion. The leaderless legion was then destroyed (Dio 71.2.1; Lucian, *Alexander the False Prophet* 27; *How to Write History* 21, 25–26). Cappadocia's regular legions, *XII Fulminata* and *XV Apollinaris*, are known to have survived long after AD 161 and, with no other likely contenders (except, perhaps, *XXII Deiotariana*), it is tempting to identify the destroyed legion as *VIIII Hispana* (see Campbell 2010 for further discussion).

# RECRUITMENT AND TERMS OF SERVICE

## From Italians to Provincials

During the Pyrrhic and Hannibalic Wars the manpower of Italy seemed inexhaustible. Pyrrhus despaired of ever defeating the legions, for they seemed to regenerate like the heads of Hydra (Zonaras 8.4). By the middle of the 1st century AD, legionary service was no longer a requirement of citizenship and, for Italians, the prospect of spending two decades or more in a legion based in a far-off province or, worse, on the frontiers of on the wild frontiers, was not enticing, was not enticing. But for other free-born men (not necessarily Roman citizens; some were enfranchised on enlistment), the legions offered purpose, pay and prospects.

Between AD 69 and 161 the composition of the Roman legions was transformed. At the start of our period, Italians, more specifically North Italians, were still a substantial element in the legions, but they were rapidly being replaced by provincial recruits and conscripts, or by the illegitimate sons of soldiers born in the *canabae*, the civilian settlements that serviced the legionary fortresses. At least part of all new legions probably continued to be raised in Italy – for example, the original complement of *legio I Italica* was mostly of Italians of six (Roman) feet in height (Suetonius, *Nero* 19.2), and an original recruit of Domitian's *I Minervia* was from Milan (*ILS 2279*) – but the element of Italian-ness lasted for a single generation. When posted to a particular province, recruits were found locally or in those regions with a surplus of manpower, for example in Illyricum or Thrace (Mann 1963; Forni 1953; 1992, 116–41).

**LEFT**
Military decorations won by Vibius Gallus during his career as a senior centurion and camp prefect: five spears, a banner, a gold crown and two rampart crowns (left); a banner and three mural crowns (right). *ILS* 2663. (© RHC Archive)

**RIGHT**
Altar dedicated to the god Mercury in the mid- or later 2nd century AD by Italian and Norican legionaries of *VI Victrix*. Italians had become a rarity in the legions, and these men may represent an emergency draft. *RIB* I 2148. (© RHC Archive)

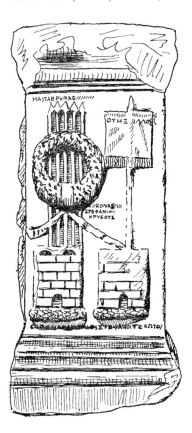
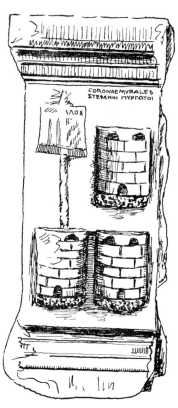

For many of these men, Latin was at best a second language, and yet the 'Roman-ness' of Germans, Pannonians, Spaniards, Africans and Syrians, fostered in the camps, was incredibly strong. Like the Italian yeomen who had battled Pyrrhus and Hannibal centuries before, the provincial legionaries were imbued with the traditional ethos of the Roman army. They were highly competitive, jealous of their honour, and driven by the need to maintain and enhance their reputations for *virtus*, that is manly courage and excellence.

## Age and class of recruits

Epitaphs suggest that most legionaries enlisted (or were conscripted) in their late teens or early 20s. However, there are some notable exceptions. A few men appear to have joined or been pressed into service in their 30s (some may have been transferred from lower-class auxiliary units and failed to mention their previous service), but more interesting are those who entered the legions at the tender age of 14.

One soldier of *legio II Adiutrix*, whose name is lost to us, died aged 25 after 11 *stipendia*, that is years of paid service (*RIB* I 481). Quintus Postunius Solus, a native of Spain, also enlisted aged 14, but not in a local legion: his 21 years of service were completed with *legio XX Valeria Victrix* in Britain (*RIB* I 502). Caecilius Donatus, another provincial recruit to *legio XX* (he was born in Thrace), enlisted aged 14. He served for 26 years, but evidently died just prior to attaining his honourable discharge (*RIB* I 523).

Legionary centurions were either men promoted from the ranks or members of the Equestrian Order who received direct commissions from the emperor. Promotion from the ranks, through the tactical grades in the century or through the administrative posts in the legion's headquarters, or a combination of both, could take many years.

Marcus Sabidius Maximus of *legio XI Claudia* was clearly numerate and literate, for he served as *signifer* (standard-bearer, also in charge of savings of the men in his century), *cornicularius* (senior clerk to the legion's commander), and then *optio* (centurion's deputy). More precisely, Maximus was an *optio ad spem ordinis*, that is a man guaranteed promotion to centurion as soon as a post became available. Maximus was finally promoted to centurion (in *legio III Gallica*) in his 20th year of service, sometime during the reign of Hadrian. Centurionates in five other legions followed and he was decorated with a *corona muralis* (wall crown) during the Bar Kochba revolt in Judaea (AD 132–135). According to Aulus Gellius, 'the mural crown is awarded by a commander to the man who is first to mount the wall and force his way into an enemy's town. It is therefore ornamented with representations of the battlements of a wall' (*Attic Nights* 5.6.16). Valiant Maximus died in his 40th year of service (*AE* 1937, 101).

At the very end of our period, Petronius Fortunatus of *legio I Italica* had a much more rapid promotion to the centurionate. Starting his career as a lowly *librarius* (clerk), he was soon promoted and over the course of four years progressed through the tactical grades in the century: *tesserarius* (officer of the watchword), *optio* and *signifer*. Then something very unusual happened. Fortunatus was promoted to centurion 'according to the vote of the legion' (*ILS* 2658). We must suppose that Fortunatus (his name means 'the fortunate') performed some exceptional feat of valour. He served in the legions for a further 46 years, winning a mural crown and a rampart crown in the Parthian War of AD 162–166.

Sextus Pilonius Modestus, an equestrian from Beneventum, received his direct commission into *legio VII Claudia Pia Fidelis* aged 18 (*ILS* 2654). One wonders how those who had risen from the ranks, like Maximus and Fortunatus, felt about such directly commissioned centurions, but Modestus was evidently a competent officer. In a career lasting 19 years, he held centurionates in five legions. He died while holding the post of *centurio hastatus posterior* (see below) of the third cohort of *legio IIII Flavia Felix*. If a directly commissioned officer was found to be lacking, he was dismissed, but in a manner that allowed him to save face: 'When the deified emperor Vespasian learned that a certain youth, of good birth, but ill adapted to military service, had received a high appointment because of his straitened circumstances, Vespasian settled a sum of money on him, and gave him an honourable discharge.' (Frontinus, *Stratagems* 4.6.4)

## Length of service

In our period, the service required of ordinary legionaries was 25 years. Perhaps only 45 per cent completed their service, either dying of wounds or diseases or being invalided out because of injuries (Scheidel 1996, 117–25). As discharge ceremonies were held only every second year, half of legionaries served 26 *stipendia*. For example, a commemorative list from Lambaesis in Numidia, the base of *legio III Augusta*, records the names and places of origin of legionaries recruited in AD 140–141 and discharged in AD 166 (*ILS* 2303). The list reveals that the many of the legion's recruits came from the towns and cities of Numidia and neighbouring provinces, but a substantial number of the men give their place of origin as *castris*, that is 'the camp'. They were the illegitimate sons of serving legionaries and local women.

The service required of ordinary legionaries was substantial (*IMS* VI 41, recording 35 years' service by a veteran of *V Alaudae* is exceptional), but the *stipendia* completed by some centurions are staggering.

It is from an inscription that we know of a vow fulfilled by Lucius Maximius Gaetulicus. In AD 127, as a new recruit of *legio XX Valeria Victrix* in Britain, he vowed to achieve the exalted rank of *primus pilus* (chief centurion). He did it, but it took 57 years! Thus, in AD 184 as *primus pilus* of *legio I Italica*

Altar dedicated to Apollo by Maximius Gaetulicus, as centurion of one of the British Legions (*RIB* I 2120). We know from another inscription that Gaetulicus was made *primus pilus* after 57 years of service! (© RHC Archive)

in Moesia, he set up a monument to the Sacred Gods of the Pantheon, as promised in his decades-old vow. Gaetulicus also prayed for the well-being of Commodus, the emperor who had finally promoted him (*AE* 1985, 753).

Gaetulicus' career is one of the longest known in the Roman army. The rank of *primus pilus* could be held for one year only. A younger man could anticipate promotion to commands of the cohorts in Rome (*vigiles* – the city of Rome's militarised fire brigade and night watch – Urban Cohorts and Praetorian Guard), the prefecture of a legion and perhaps ultimately an appointment to govern a small province. A few even became Praetorian Prefect, the second most powerful man in the Empire, but Gaetulicus was probably considered too old for further promotion.

Retonius Lucius, who also crowned his career with the primipilate (in *legio I Adiutrix*), retired after 58 years (*CIL* III 11031). Aelius Silvanus was born in Jerusalem and ended his career as a centurion in *legio II Adiutrix*. He holds the record for the longest service in the Roman army: 61 years. He died aged 86, a real senior centurion (*Tit. Aq.* II 499).

## Pay and pension

At the start of our period, the basic annual pay of the legionary was 900 *sestertii*. The *stipendium*, as it was known, was paid in three instalments over the course of the year. Legionary cavalrymen (*equites*), with higher equipment and fodder costs, received 1,050 *sestertii*. The centurions of cohorts II–X each received about 13,500 *sestertii*. The senior centurions of the first cohort (*primi ordines*) received far more – 27,000 *sestertii*. The *primus pilus* earned a huge amount: 54,000 *sestertii*.

In AD 84, Domitian added a fourth instalment to the *stipendium* and so increased basic pay to 1,200 *sestertii* per year (Suetonius, *Domitian* 7.3). The pay rates of *equites* and higher ranks were increased accordingly: *equites* receiving 1,400 *sestertii*; centurions 18,000; *primi ordines* 36,000; and the *primus pilus* 72,000.

Under-officers (*principales*) received higher rates of pay. *Sesquiplicarii*, such as the *tesserarius*, earned 50 per cent above the basic rate. Senior *principales*, like the *optio*, *signifer* and *cornicularius*, were *duplicarii*, that is men on double pay.

Automatic deductions were made for clothing, equipment, rations and fodder and religious festivals, and a fixed sum had to be deposited in the legion's savings bank (administered by the standard-bearers), but it seems that the legionary could live fairly comfortably on what remained (M. A. Speidel 1992).

Centurions (note vine stick and swords worn on the left) on a metope of the Tropaeum Traiani. A centurion received 15 times more pay than an ordinary legionary. *Primi ordines* earned even more. (© C. Chirita)

On discharge, the legionary received a lump-sum pension or a plot of land (cf. Tacitus, *Annals* 1.17). In our period, Vespasian was active in the establishment of veterans' colonies, especially in southern Italy, but it seems that most legionaries preferred to receive cash *praemia* and set up home in the vicinity of their legion's fortress, or perhaps return to their place of birth. In AD 5, the emperor Augustus set the *praemium* for an ordinary legionary at 12,000 *sestertii* (cf. Dio 55.23.1). It is not known if his successors increased this basic amount, but soldiers of higher rank got more. During the reign of Domitian, an *armidoctor* (see below), received a gratuity of 30,000 *sestertii* (*AE* 1952, 153).

### Belief and belonging

Titus Valerius Marcianus was born in the camp of *legio V Macedonica* at Troesmis (or rather the civilian settlement beside it), and recruited into his father's legion in AD 145. In the latter part of his career, he saw considerable active service. He participated in the Parthian War of AD 162–166, and in the early campaigns of the Marcomannic Wars. After he was discharged in Dacia in AD 170, he settled in the vicinity of the camp at Troesmis (*ILS* 2311). He was born in the shadow of the camp, and he would die beside it.

'The soldier's pride is in his camp. It is his country, his home.' So wrote Tacitus (*Histories* 3.84), who knew, probably from first-hand experience as a *tribunus laticlavius*, of the ties that bound legionaries together. And if the camp was home, comrades were family: the legionaries referred to themselves as brothers (e.g. *AE* 1991, 1114; MacMullen 1984, 43). Love for the legion bound them together. The legion itself had a sacred spirit, a *numen* or *genius* (Tacitus, *Annals* 2.17; *ILS* 2295). It resided in the *aquila*, the eagle standard. Each century, too, possessed a *genius*, represented by its standard. The legionaries followed the standards into battle, died to protect them, and sacrificed to them in the event of victory (Josephus, *Jewish War* 6.225, 316).

# TRAINING

The Romans knew their army as the *exercitus*. The literal meaning of this Latin word is 'exercise' and it emphasizes the importance placed on training and discipline. The emperor Hadrian, a former legionary tribune and legate, insisted on a vigorous training regime. 'He kept the soldiers in training as if war were imminent' (Historia Augusta, *Hadrian* 10.2) and 'drilled the men in every kind of battle' (Dio 69.9.3, cf. Arrian, *Tactica* 44 on Hadrian requiring Roman cavalry to practise Parthian, Armenian and Sarmatian bow and lance fighting techniques).

### Armatura

The Romans believed that intensive training could turn raw recruits into steadfast fighters. According to Cicero, training 'produces the spirit prepared to face wounds in battle. Bring forward a soldier of equal courage, but untrained, he will seem a mere woman' (*Tusculan Disputations* 2.37). The basic training of the legionary recruit is described in *RL* 11–12. Thereafter the legionary practised his weapons drill (with *pilum* and *gladius*) on a daily basis (Vegetius 2.23 and Josephus, *Jewish War* 3.73).

One particular drill was the *armatura*. According to Vegetius, it was a special weapons drill and those who mastered it could outfight any other troops (1.13, 2.14). Legionaries with the rank of *armatura* were probably instructors of this drill (cf. Speidel 2006, 76). Lucius Calpurnius Concitatus, an *armatura* of *legio IIII Flavia Felix*, bore a name rather appropriate for such an instructor. In Latin, *concitatus* means swift, energetic and violent (*CIL* III 1663). In the early 3rd century AD, *legio II Adiutrix* had enough *armaturae* to form a *collegium* ('association', *ILS* 2363), but we can only guess at how many *armatura* instructors were in a legion. One per cohort or even one per century?

A long period of service was required before a man was considered for the role of *armatura*. Staberius Felix, a soldier of *legio VII Gemina*, served for 12 years before he became *discens armaturae*, a trainee instructor (*AE* 1991, 1114). Another weapons instructor was the *armidoctor*. After completing his service in the Praetorian Guard (nominally 16 years) in the middle of the 1st century AD, Lucius Pellartius Celer was retained by an emperor as an *evocatus*, and then made *armidoctor* of *legio XV Apollinaris*. Celer was eventually discharged by the emperor Domitian, after 43 years of service (*AE* 1952, 153).

## Campidoctores

It is uncertain how often the legionary century went through its battle manoeuvres, whether as an individual unit, as part of its cohort, battle line or with the complete legion. It may be that practice in battle formations and manoeuvres were part of thrice (or more) monthly route marches (Vegetius 1.27).

Josephus emphasizes that Roman field exercises were very realistic. 'Hence the ease with which they sustain the shock of battle... Their training manoeuvres are bloodless battles, and their battles bloody manoeuvres' (*Jewish War* 3.74–76).

The officer responsible for exercises on the parade ground (*campus*) was probably the *campidoctor* ('field instructor'). Evidence from other units of the Imperial army indicates varying grades of *campidoctor*, from high-ranking centurions who could direct the training of a complete unit (e.g. *ILS* 2416, notably a dedication to Mars of the Parade Ground), to those responsible for training at the level of the century (*CIL* VI 2697, a legionary transferred to the Praetorian Guard). In the Praetorian Guard, *campidoctores* were drawn from the ranks of the *doctores* (*ILS* 2088). These *doctores* were probably specialist weapons instructors (e.g. *CIL* VI 3595, *doctor sagittarum* –

**TRAINING AT LAMBAESIS, AD 128**

Legionaries of *III Augusta* fight a mock battle on their training ground at Lambaesis in AD 128. The emperor Hadrian, on one of his regular tours of inspection, looks on from a tribunal. We know from an inscription that Hadrian, a former legionary commander, addressed the soldiers and critiqued their efforts. His speech also suggests that the battle order of the legion may have been similar to the famous *triplex acies* (triple battle line) of the manipular legions of the Republic (Speidel 2006).

Here we see two centuries advancing rapidly (the *concursus*) into javelin range. The legionaries hurl their dummy wooden *pila*, draw their wooden practice swords (cf. Vegetius 1.11) and then charge (the *impetus*), seeking to collide with and topple their opponents. Each century is led by a centurion and standard-bearer. The centurions are distinguished by the transverse crests on their helmets, but it may be that the crest fell out of use in the later 1st century AD.

an archery instructor). Despite the emphasis placed on discipline, Roman legionaries could be unruly, disobedient and sometimes mutinous. But even after a period of dissipation, the lessons of the centurions, *campidoctores* and *armaturae* were not forgotten.

On 17 September AD 69, Aulus Caecina Alienus, general of the emperor Vitellius, marched north from Rome to intercept the Flavian forces led by Marcus Antonius Primus, legate of *legio VII Gemina*. However, Alienus fretted about the state of his army.

> Alienus reached Cremona and occupied the town, but seeing that his own soldiers were out of training as a result of their luxurious life in Rome and impaired by a lack of drilling, whereas the Flavians were well exercised in body and stout of heart, he felt afraid. Later, when friendly proposals came to him from Primus, he called the soldiers together, and by pointing out the weakness of Vitellius and the strength of Vespasian, as well as the character of the two men, he persuaded them to change sides. So at the time they removed the images of Vitellius from their standards and took an oath that they would be ruled by Vespasian. But after the meeting had broken up and they had retired to their tents, they changed their minds and suddenly, rushing together in great haste and excitement, they again saluted Vitellius as emperor and imprisoned Alienus for having betrayed them, showing no reverence even for his consular office [18 October]. Such things are, in fact, characteristic of civil wars.
> Dio 65.10.2–4

So Vitellius' legions embarked on the second battle of Cremona without a general to direct them. Of course, the army still had its legates, prefects, tribunes, centurions and drill instructors, and despite their excesses in Rome, and apparent lack of drill, the Vitellian legionaries were all fully trained and experienced Roman soldiers.

> The battle [fought over the night of 24–25 October] was not the result of any definite plan. Some few horsemen, as often happens when two forces are encamped opposite each other, suddenly attacked some of the enemy's foragers, and then reinforcements came to both parties from their respective armies, just as these happened to become aware of the situation, first to one side, then to the other, now of one kind of fighting force, now of another, both infantry and cavalry; and the conflict was marked by the usual vicissitudes until all had hastened to the front. Then they [the Vitellians] got into some kind of regular formation, as if a signal had been given, and carried on the struggle with some order, even though leaderless; for Alienus had been imprisoned at Cremona.
> Dio 65.11.4–5

# THE TACTICAL ORGANIZATION OF THE LEGION

The basic organization of the cohortal legion of the Late Republic and Early Empire is clear enough, but many problems remain concerning tactical functions and deployment. The difficulties mean that, for this section, we must expand our focus to include evidence from the Middle and Late Republican eras, and even the Late Empire.

## The size of the legion

The exact size of an Early Imperial legion is not known. It is clear that the legion was divided into ten cohorts. There were six centuries in a cohort, each commanded by a centurion with the following titles:

pilus prior
pilus posterior
princeps prior
princeps posterior
hastatus prior
hastatus posterior

In some legions, the first cohort may have had double-sized centuries (Hyginus, *On the Fortifications of the Camp* 21). The fragmentary inscribed lists of men recruited into *legio VII Claudia* in AD 169, and honourably discharged in AD 195, were thought to support the existence of a first cohort of double strength. The fragments suggested that 47 legionaries were discharged from the first cohort, twice or even three times the number released from any other cohort (*CIL* III 14507). However, the discovery of another fragment increased to 39 the number of men discharged from the legion's seventh cohort (Mirkovic 2004, 212–13). It is most unlikely that the seventh cohort was of double strength. We must conclude that in *VII Claudia*, and probably in most other legions, the first cohort was no larger than cohorts II–X.

As the rank of *pilus posterior* is missing from the majority of inscriptions referring to the first cohort, it is often assumed that the cohort had only five centuries and therefore five centuries. However, the number was probably six. Tacitus refers the six *primi ordines* ('first rankers'), that is the centurions

Memorial to Pompeius Asper, whose career saw him progress from centurion to chief centurion and ultimately camp prefect, the third in command of a legion. *ILS* 2662. (© RHC Archive)

of the first cohort, of *legio VII Galbiana* being killed at the second battle of Cremona in AD 69 (*Histories* 3.22), and the 'missing' rank of *centurio pilus posterior* is found in the first cohort of one legion – *II Parthica* (*AE* 1993, 1588). In AD 161, *legio III Augusta* had no fewer than seven centurions in its first cohort, including two *primi pili* ('chief centurions'; *ILS* 2452). At least one of the seven centurions was a supernumerary, but the title of the second chief centurion could be expanded to *primus pilus posterior*.

Given that a legionary century numbered 80 men (below), a cohort was therefore 480 strong, and a legion 4,800. With the addition of 120 cavalry (Josephus, *Jewish War* 3.120), 60 centurions, the legate (senatorial commander), six tribunes (one senatorial and nominally second in command, and five of equestrian rank), the camp prefect (third in command, a former senior centurion elevated to equestrian rank), and some supernumerary officers, the complement of a legion was approximately 5,000. However, a full-strength legion was something of a rare beast.

## The size of the century

According to Hyginus, the legionary *centuria* (century) of the Early Empire numbered 80 soldiers (*On the Fortifications of the Camp* 1). More precisely, Hyginus says a *plena centuria*, that is a full century, had 80 men, which may be taken as an indication that army units were often well below their ideal paper strengths. Hyginus did not include the centurion in this figure; thus a full century on the battlefield numbered 81 men.

Despite their rank and status, it seems clear from Hyginus' description of the space allocated to a century in his ideal fortified camp, that the *principales* ('foremost' or 'best men') of the century, namely the *signifer*, *optio* and *tesserarius*, were included among the 80 legionaries, and had to share tents with the *milites gregarii*, the common soldiers. The centurion certainly did not share his double-sized tent (*papilio*) with the under-officers; like his suite of rooms in the legionary barracks, this spacious tent was a privilege of rank.

## The *contubernium*

Hyginus tells us that eight legionaries shared a tent, making for ten *contubernia*, that is mess and tent groups, per century (*On the Fortifications of the Camp* 1). In the 4th century AD, a larger *contubernium* of ten soldiers was commanded by an under-officer known as the *decanus*, 'the commander of ten', or the *caput contubernii*, 'head of the *contubernium*' (Vegetius 2.8, 13).

It is tempting to assume that these under-officers acted as file leaders in battle; compare the role of infantry file leaders and decarchs – the equivalent of Vegetius' *decani* – in the Roman army of the late 6th century AD (Maurice, *Strategicon* 12.b.9). However, in the era of the classic cohortal legion, that is *c*.100 BC – AD 300, there is no convincing evidence for legionary *contubernium* commanders, or that the *contubernium* was a tactical subunit of the century. An inscription on a hand-mill from Saalburg records that it belonged to con(tubernium) Brittonis, or 'the contubernium of Britto', but Britto's function was probably administrative and logistical (*CIL* XIII 11954a). He was the 'leader' of his mess and tent group, for that is what the contubernium was. He was not the commander of a tactical subunit.

Tombstone of Valerius Pudens of *legio II Adiutrix*. He is identified by his century (that of Dossennius Proculus, lines 6–7), not by *contubernium*. Note the dolphins and trident motif, perhaps an allusion to the naval origins of the legion. *ILS* 2278. (© RHC Archive)

When describing the organization of the Roman cavalry *turma* (squadron) of the middle of the 2nd century BC, Polybius says the 30-man unit was led by three *decuriones* ('commanders of tens'), who were supported by three *ouragoi* ('file closers'), meaning *optiones*. The *decuriones* were not equal in rank; one had overall command of the complete *turma* (Polybius 6.25.1–2).

The situation was similar in the infantry maniple, the smallest tactical subunit of Polybius' legion. Of the two centurions, the senior was probably in overall charge of the complete maniple, not just his half of it (Polybius 6.24.1, 7–9). However, unlike the *turma*, the maniple was not subdivided into smaller tactical subunits. It was led by two centurions, but it was not divided into two *centuriae*. The duplication of officers and under-officers (*optiones* and standard bearers) was to ensure that it was 'never to be without a leader and chief' (Polybius 6.24.7–9).

Polybius never mentions centuries or other subdivisions of the maniple (Isaac 1998, 389). The smallest tactical infantry unit of the legion in the Middle Republic was therefore the maniple of 120 or 160 men (and only 60 in the maniples of the veteran *triarii*), whereas the smallest tactical cavalry unit was the *decuria* of ten men. We do not know why the Romans felt it necessary to subdivide the small cavalry unit but not the larger maniple. The lack of tactical subdivision in the infantry may seem surprising, but the situation continued into the Imperial period, until at least the close of the 3rd century AD.

The *contubernia* of the legionary century were not tactical subunits and almost certainly did not form files in the battle line. It has been suggested that *immunes*, that is soldiers exempted from the more unpleasant and onerous duties on account of performing specialist functions, could have had command of the *contubernia* (Goldsworthy 1996, 14). In the extensive literary, epigraphic and papyrological sources relating to the Roman army of the Early Empire, there is no mention of a *contubernium* commander of the sort described by Vegetius. Professor Benjamin Isaac has stressed that the *contubernium* 'appears to have been an arrangement for the barracks only, for it is not reflected in the composition of the officer corps' (Isaac 1998, 400).

If there were *contubernium* commanders in the Early Empire we would expect the epitaphs of ordinary *munifices* (legionaries without specialisms who had to perform fatigues) to mention their *contubernium* commanders, but they refer only to centurions or the titles of their centuries. The epitaph of Lucius Silicius Saturninus of *legio III Augusta* is typical. It informs us that 'he was killed in action under the centurion Lucilius, between Aras and Vatari [in Numidia]' (*ILS* 9088).

We do not find examples of *contubernium* commanders in our period, because the rank did not exist. Just as the maniple was the smallest tactical unit of the Middle Republican legion, the century was the smallest tactical unit of the Late Republican and Early Imperial legions.

The *caput contubernii* was a creation of the late 3rd or 4th century AD. The gravestone of Flavius Ziper of the *numerus I Martia Victrix* (perhaps identical with the *legio I Martia* established at the close of the 3rd century AD by the emperor Diocletian), gives him the abbreviated rank of *CAP*. This has been restored as *caput*, perhaps indicating the 'head' of a *contubernium* (*AE* 1891, 102), but by then the organization of the legion was becoming quite different. The move from formations based on ranks to formations composed of files (as found in Maurice's *Strategicon*) is probably important, and transformed the mess-group leader into a file leader on the battlefield.

## Ranks and files

When in an unusually close formation like the *cuneus* (attack column) or *testudo* ('tortoise', a formation with walls and roof of shields) we can assume that legionaries were arranged in files, but their regular battle field order seems to have been in staggered open ranks appropriate to javelin and sword fighters. According to Polybius:

> In the case of the Romans each soldier with his arms also occupies a space of three feet in breadth [the same as a Macedonian phalangite], but as in their mode of fighting each man must move separately, as he has to cover his person with his long shield, turning to meet each expected blow, and as he uses his sword both for cutting and thrusting it is obvious that a looser order is required, and each man must be at a distance of at least three feet from the man next him in the same rank and those in front of and behind him, if they are to be of proper use The consequence will be that one Roman must stand opposite two men in the first rank of the phalanx, so that he has to face and encounter ten pikes, and it is both impossible for a single man to cut through them all in time once they are at close quarters and by no means easy to force their points away, as the rear ranks can be of no help to the front rank either in thus forcing the pikes away or in the use of the sword.
> Polybius 18.30.6–10

With each legionary occupying 6 or 7ft of space, we would assume that the legionary in the following rank was positioned to cover the interval of 3ft in front of him, thus resulting in staggered ranks. He would also avoid being injured when the legionary in the forward rank drew back his arm to throw his *pilum*. Vegetius allocated the legionary three feet within the rank and increased the space between ranks to 6ft (3.14–15). Polybius' evidence is to be preferred.

**LEGIONARY CAVALRYMAN, AD 161**

The small cavalry element of the Imperial legion is often overlooked. Only 120 troopers strong (Josephus, *Jewish War* 3.120), its organization is not well understood. The cavalrymen were drawn from, and continued to be identified, by the infantry centuries in which they were originally enrolled. Until the 2nd century BC, legionary cavalry was organised in *turmae*, but in our era, there is curiously no evidence for such tactical subdivision.

The cavalry possessed important under-officers – standard-bearer (*vexillarius*), *tesserarius* and *optio*, but we do not hear of a commanding officer. Perhaps the function was performed by a tribune or a supernumerary centurion.

The reconstruction shows a legionary trooper (**1**) in a semi-rigid scale cuirass with embossed chest plates (after finds from Mušov and Manching), full-length greaves with hinged knee guards (Regensburg), and a so-called cavalry sports helmet based on an example of unknown provenance in the Getty Museum. The iron helmet (**2**) of Robinson's Auxiliary Cavalry type E, is probably more typical of the variety of helmet used in battle. The legionary's sword follows an example from Canterbury. It has an unusually long tang for a Roman sword, hence the hand-and-a-half hilt shown here. The flat oval shield is well known from triumphal monuments and the gravestones of cavalrymen. A simple wreath device has been selected as the blazon because it seems the classic lightning bolt motif had fallen out of use.

The horse's studded leather chamfron and harness decorations follow finds from Newstead. The inserts show much more decorative examples of metallic horse armour from Straubing (**3**), perhaps more often used for cavalry displays but, like the masked helmet, not necessarily unfamiliar to the battle field. The inserts also show the four-horned Roman saddle, and how it held the legionary firmly in place (**4**). Such a saddle meant that despite lacking stirrups, Roman horseman had a stable fighting platform and could perform as 'shock' cavalry in combat.

1

2

3

4

With the armament of the legionary remaining essentially the same in the Late Republic and Early Empire, that is heavy javelin or dual-purpose thrusting and throwing spear, large shield and cut-and-thurst sword, we can reasonably assume that Polybius' open order remained the standard deployment for the century of the later 1st and 2nd centuries AD.

### Veterans in the front rank

Like the maniple, the legionary century had no need for under-officers with the rank or function of file leader, but there is some evidence for the positioning of veterans in the front rank.

1. The battle of Pistoria (62 BC) provides an unequivocal example. The rebel Catiline formed the leading rank, maybe even the complete first battle line, of his army from *evocati*. These veterans had previously served under him or Sulla and were recalled to service (*evocatio*) on account of their experience and courage (Sallust, *War With Catilina* 59.3, 61.2–3).

2. Pompey's army at Pharsalus (48 BC) included some 2,000 *evocati* (Caesar, *Civil War* 3.88). They were veterans of Pompey's campaigns in Spain, Italy and the Near East – men like Titus Flavius Petro of Raete, the ancestor of the emperor Vespasian (Suetonius, *Vespasian* 1.2). It may be that these *evocati* formed the front rank of Pompey's army and bravely resisted the *pila* volley and running charge (*impetus*) of Caesar's legionaries (*Civil War* 3.93). That they had the nerve to hold their ground in the face of such a terrifying assault points to considerable prior experience of combat.

Valerius Crispus of *legio VIII Augusta* died in his 21st year of service. With so many years of experience, he may have fought in the front rank. *CIL* XIII 7574. (© RHC Archive)

3. When Titus Labienus surrounded Caesar's army of five newly levied legions at Ruspina (46 BC), he rode up to taunt the frightened recruits but a veteran, formerly of the Tenth Legion, stepped out of the front rank and killed Labienus' horse with his *pilum* (Anonymous, *African War* 16). The episode suggests that the new legions were formed around cadres of veterans and that the experienced soldiers were positioned in the leading ranks, where the fighting was hardest.

We can suppose that it was usual to position the best soldiers in the front rank of the century and that the practice continued under the Empire. Epigraphic evidence records young and mature legionaries of the Early Empire who were killed in combat. For example, Vibius Felix of *legio III Augusta* was aged 21, and only 13 months into his legionary service, when he was killed somewhere in Numidia 'in an armed encounter with the enemy' (*CIL* VIII 3275). Lucius Flaminius, a native of Carthage, was 21 when 'chosen in the *dilectus* (levy) of Marcus Silanus' (i.e. sometime in the AD 30s). Flaminius served for 19 years until he was cut down, aged 40, in a skirmish at a *praesidium* (garrison post) in the Saltus Philomusianus (*ILS* 2305).

The epitaphs of Felix and Flaminius preserve much useful information but, considering that both men were killed in minor engagements, do not help resolve the question about who made up the front ranks of the legions in major pitched battles in the first and second centuries ad. It is worth quoting here Tacitus' tale of Iulius Mansuetus, a veteran serving in a Vitellian legion, at the second battle of Cremona:

Iulius Mansuetus, a Spaniard, enlisting in the legion [*XXI*] *Rapax*, had left at home a son of tender age. The lad grew up to manhood, and was conscripted by Galba into the Seventh Legion. Now chancing to meet his father, he brought him to the ground with a wound, and, as he rifled his dying foe, recognized him, and was himself recognized. Clasping the expiring man in his arms, in piteous cries he implored the spirit of his father to be propitious to him, and not to turn from him with loathing as from a parricide. 'This guilt,' he said, 'is shared by all; how small a part of a civil war is a single soldier!' With these words he raised the body, opened a grave, and discharged the last duties for his father. This was noticed by those who were on the spot, then by many others; astonishment and indignation ran through the whole army, and they cursed this most horrible war. Yet as eagerly as ever they stripped the bodies of slaughtered kinsmen, relatives, and brothers. They talk of an impious act having been done, and they do it themselves.

Tacitus, *Histories* 3.25

This grim episode may point to recently recruited legionaries being in the front ranks. It occurred, however, during the pursuit of the broken Vitellians. Tacitus' source for this incident was Vipstanus Messalla, another veteran of the battle. This young senatorial tribune was temporarily in command of the Flavian *legio VII Claudia* (cf. *Histories* 3.9).

The specialist functions of certain legionaries would suggest they fought in the front ranks. *Armaturae* would presumably have been among the fore fighters. Saturninus, an *armatura* of *legio II Adiutrix*, was killed in Dacia aged 34, after 16 years of service (*CIL* III 3336). *Campidoctores* certainly fought in the front rank. In AD 359, the famous night attack on the siege camp of Shapur II at Amida was led by legionary *campidoctores* (Ammianus Marcellinus 19.6.12). In war, *armidoctores*, too, must have led by example. Pellartius Celer, weapons instructor of *legio XV Apollinaris*, was awarded with a *corona aurea* ('gold crown') and other decorations for his conspicuous valour in the Jewish War (*AE* 1952, 153), perhaps received at Jerusalem in AD 70.

## File closers and *optiones*

In the Macedonian phalanxes of the Hellenistic kingdoms, file leaders led attacks and file closers made sure the soldiers in the intervening ranks did not get out of step, falter or attempt to flee:

We shall place the strongest in the front rank and behind them the most intelligent, and of the former the file leaders (*lochagoi*) shall be those who excel in size, strength and skill. This line of file leaders binds the phalanx together and is like the cutting edge of the sword… The second line must also be not much inferior to the first, so that when a file leader falls his comrade behind may move forward and hold the line together. The file closers (*ouragoi*), both those in the files and those attached to larger units, should be men who surpass the rest in presence of mind, the former to hold their own files straight, the latter to keep the divisions in file and rank with one another besides bringing back to position any who may leave their places through fear, and forcing them to close up in case they lock shields.

Asclepiodotus, *Tactics* 3.5–6

The heavy infantry formations of the Roman army of the late 6th century AD relied on under-officers with functions identical to the *lochagoi* and *ouragoi* (Maurice, *Strategicon* 12.b.9, 16, 17). However, such under-officers seem to be lacking in the legions of the period *c*.100 BC – AD 300. For example, when Caesar's army was ambushed by the Nervii at the River Sabis (57 BC), frightened soldiers in the rear ranks of the Twelfth Legion had little difficulty fleeing (Caesar, *Gallic War* 2.25). There were evidently no file closers to shove them back into the ranks. What about the *optiones* of the centuries?

It is from Polybius' use of the Greek title *ouragos*, literally meaning 'tail man', to indicate the *optio* (Latin for 'helper' or 'assistant') of the centurion, that we tend to assume he was positioned in, or behind, the rear rank of the maniple or century (Polybius 6.24.2).

Professor Michael P. Speidel has noted that some gravestones of legionary *optiones* show the deceased holding long staffs. From our specific period, the best examples are the memorials of Caecilius Avitus of *legio XX Valeria Victrix* (*RIB* 492) and Aelius Mestrius of *legio II Adiutrix* (*CIL* III 3530; set up by his fellow *optiones*). Some later *tesserarii* are depicted with similar long staffs. Take, for example, the funerary monuments of two *tesserarii* of *legio II Parthica* at Apamea in Syria. Aurelius Celsus died during the Persian War of AD 231–233 and his gravestone shows him holding a staff decorated with horizontal stripes. Aurelius Ingenuus died during the next Persian War (AD 242–244), and his gravestone depicts him holding the writing tablets he used to distribute the watch word (*tessera*) and a long staff (*AE* 1993, 1585 and 1588). Ingenuus' epitaph is also notable for recording that he served in the century of the *pilus posterior* of the first cohort, the centurion missing from the corps of the *primi ordines* in other legions.

The vine stick (*vitis*) was symbolic of the centurion's rank (and of the *evocatus*, cf. Dio 55.24.8), and the *beneficiarius* had his distinctive lance. It seems likely that the long staff was the insignia of the *optio* and *tesserarius*. Speidel proposes that the staffs of the *optiones* were practical as well as symbolic.

Highlighting passages in Maurice's *Strategicon*, where the file closers shove the ranks in front of them along, keep the files straight and prevent frightened soldiers from attempting to flee (12.b.16 and 17), Speidel suggests that *optiones* were positioned just behind the rear ranks and employed their staffs to shove soldiers back into formation (Speidel 1992, 24–26). If we accept Speidel's proposal, we could also locate the *tesserarii* to the rear of the centuries, where they would assist the *optiones* in keeping order in the ranks.

However, the *Strategicon* informs us that file closers would use their spears to prod soldiers disobeying the order to keep silent. It does not tell us that spears or staffs were used to force back-stepping and frightened soldiers into formation. We can imagine that the shields of the file closers were most effective for shoving soldiers forward. Moreover, we do not actually know if *optiones* and *tesserarii* of the Early Empire carried their staffs into battle. Aelius Septimus, an *optio* of *legio I Adiutrix*, was slain during the Marcomannic Wars. His gravestone shows him wielding a sword and shield in battle. One German lies dead at Septimus' feet, and another collapses with a mortal wound (*CIL* III 10969; *RBT* 49).

As the centurion's deputy, it is natural to assume that the *optio* took command of the century if the centurion was killed or seriously wounded. (Vegetius 2.7 tells us that the *optio* took charge when the centurion fell ill). Returning to the battle of the Sabis, the ease with which some of Caesar's legionaries peeled away from the rear ranks may be explained because the *optiones* had moved to the front of their centuries to replace the dead centurions (Caesar, *Gallic War* 2.25). However, if the *optio* was expected to assume command, would it not be more practical for him to be positioned closer to the centurion?

In Livy's account of the battle of the Veseris (340 BC), a *subcenturio* ('under-centurion', probably an *optio*) fights in the front rank because his aged centurion had been killed by a Latin *primus pilus* (Livy 8.8.18). The memorial to the *optio* Aelius Septimus (above), if not a generic scene of triumph, but an attempt to accurately portray his part in the battle in which he fell, suggests he fought at the front of his century.

Portrait of an unknown centurion, identified by his *vitis* (vine stick) in Graz. Note the oval shield. (© IKAI)

Legionaries may actually have expected the standard-bearer, their visual focus for direction and movement (and, in *turmae*, the leader of manoeuvres, cf. Arrian, *Tactica* 36.6), to take command if the centurion fell. In fact, the standard-bearer was senior in rank to the regular *optio* (but not to the *optio ad spem ordinis*). Standard-bearers were clearly located in the front rank (e.g. Anonymous, *African War* 15–18). Like centurions, their place at the front of the century, their essential tactical function, and the prize value of their standards, made them an obvious target for the enemy and their casualties were always heavy.

The *tesserarius* may have been found in the front or forward ranks. The *Strategicon* demonstrates that in the Late Roman army, officers were placed on the right and left flanks of the leading rank (3.2–4), perhaps to lead the formation in wheeling manoeuvres, and most probably to ensure the cohesion of the flanks. We can speculate that the *tesserarius* may have performed such a function, but there is no supportive evidence in the sources.

### Where did the centurion stand?

The centurion was positioned in the front rank of the century (cf. Sallust, *War With Catilina* 59.3). Fighting in the front rank took a heavy toll. Theoretically, one centurion should have been killed for every 80 legionary casualties, but they suffered disproportionately high losses because they led by example and covered retreats.

The best known example of heavy losses is the battle of Gergovia (52 BC), where 46 centurions and 700 legionaries were killed; one centurion for every 15 legionaries (Caesar, *Gallic War* 7.51). At Pharsalus, the casualties of Caesar's centurions were incredibly disproportionate: 30 centurions and 200 legionaries killed (Caesar, *Civil War* 3.99). When Mithridates VI of Pontus

routed the army of Gaius Triarius at Zela (67 BC), 150 centurions were killed. Assuming Triarius led four legions, the casualty rate of the centurions was almost 50 per cent (Plutarch, *Lucullus* 35.2; Appian, *Mithridatic Wars* 89). At Pistoria (62 BC), it seems that all of Catiline's centurions were killed: 'Almost every man covered with his body, when life was gone, the position which he had taken when alive at the beginning of the conflict. A few, indeed, in the centre, whom the praetorian cohort had scattered, lay a little apart from the rest, but the wounds even of these were in front.' (Sallust, *War With Catiline* 61.2–3).

In other battles, we hear of all the centurions of a cohort being killed. At the Sabis (57 BC), all six centurions of the fourth cohort of Caesar's *legio XII* were killed (Caesar, *Gallic War* 2.25). At Dyrrachium (48 BC), all the *primi ordines* of a Caesarian legion, except for the *princeps prior*, were slain in a furious fight to save their legion's eagle. The eagle was saved, but its *aquilifer* (eagle bearer) died of his wounds (Caesar, *Civil War* 3.64). That little had changed in our period is confirmed by the casualties sustained by *legio VII Galbiana* at the second battle of Cremona in AD 69: the recently formed legion lost all of its *primi ordines* (Tacitus, *Histories* 3.22).

Were casualty rates among centurions so high because they actually stood slightly apart from their centuries? Modern reconstructions of the *centuria* tend to place the centurion in an exposed position to the right of the first rank, and he is usually separated from his standard-bearer and trumpeter. See, for example, Peter Connolly's classic reconstruction of an imperial legion on parade (Connolly 1975, 40–41 = 2006, 216–17). One wonders if this famous illustration influenced Dr Adrian Goldsworthy's proposal that 'perhaps the centurion stood slightly ahead and to the right (the right being the natural side of offensive action) of the front rank' (Goldsworthy 1996, 182).

Polybius tells us 'when both centurions were present, the first elected centurion commands the right half of the maniple and the second the left, but if both are not present the one who is commands the whole' (6.24.8).

The *crista transversa* depicted on the gravestone of Calidius Severus, centurion of *legio XV Apollinaris*. The distinctive transverse crest may have gone out of use in the later 1st century AD. *ILS* 2596. (© Florian Himmler)

Polybius' description might suggest that the centurions stood, respectively, at the extreme right and left of the first rank of the maniple. Xenophon, the Athenian soldier, emphasized that being the leader of a flank file was dangerous enough, but to actually stand apart from the formation was suicidal (*Education of Cyrus* 2.2.6–9). Of course, Greek hoplite warfare, in which maintenance of the close order of phalanx was paramount, was quite different to the individualistic combat preferred by the Romans.

A diagram in the *Strategicon* shows a cavalry *tagma* (regiment) of 310 troopers with the commander located at the centre of the front rank. To the immediate right of the commander is the unit's standard-bearer, and in the rank behind him is the trumpeter. The commander's cape bearer (a senior orderly) is also close at hand (Maurice, *Strategicon* 3.2). This seems a very sensible arrangement. The commander can lead from the front, but is not exposed on a flank. He is not separated from his essential tools of command and control, namely the standard for giving visual signals (by its location at the centre, the standard should be visible to the whole unit), and the trumpet for the transmission of audible signals.

If we take the position of the cavalry command group in *Strategicon* 3.2 and apply it to the maniple in Polybius 6.24.8, this would result in the two centurions being positioned at the centres of their respective halves of the maniple. (*Strategicon* 12.b.11 implies that the commander of the infantry *tagma*, and his standard bearer, were also positioned at the front centre of the battle formation.)

At the close of the 2nd century BC, the maniple was split into two centuries. If we continue to use the *Strategicon* as a guide, the centurion of the *centuria* would have taken up his station in the middle of the front rank, an excellent position from which to lead his unit forward. Generally, legionary centuries were not expected to do much more than advance forward (the *concursus*), pause for the *pila* volley, charge at the run (the *impetus*), and then collide with the enemy and hack and slash with swords until exhausted. The lines would then separate briefly until the legionaries gathered themselves to resume the fight (Caesar, *Civil War* 3.93 and Appian, *Civil Wars* 3.68). Complex manoeuvres were rare in Roman battles, and the units that performed them were normally prepared in advance.

In the front central position, the centurion was well placed for his soldiers to identify him by his *crista transversa* – transverse crest. Vegetius informs us that the crest (which was, according to him, silvered) acted as another *signum* (standard) for the legionaries to follow (2.13, 16). However, depictions of the transverse crest on the funerary monuments of centurions are surprisingly rare and the crest is nowhere to be seen on Trajan's Column or, more importantly, on the metopes of the Tropaeum Traiani at Adamclisi, which were produced by legionary sculptors. This suggests that the crest had gone out of use by the end of the 1st century AD (Durry 1928, 305–08).

## Horn-players and trumpeters

In AD 203, 35 or 36 *cornicines* (horn players) of *legio III Augusta* dedicated a monument to the good fortune and safety of the Imperial family, and outlined the financial benefits for members of their *collegium* (*ILS* 2354). If 35/6 was the total number of horn players in the legion (by no means certain – others could have belonged to a different club), it would suggest that only half of the legion's centuries possessed a *cornicen*; the five or six extra musicians could be explained as trainees (*discentes*) or as supernumeraries. The legion's 30 other centuries may have had *tubicines* (trumpeters) to sound the signals. Both instruments could be used to signal the order to assume battle formation or to attack (Anonymous, *African War* 82; Tacitus, *Annals* 1.68).

**LEFT**
Detail of the *cornu* of Aurelius Bitus, *cornicen* of *legio II Adiutrix*. As it required both hands to play the horn, his small shield appears to be suspended. *CIL* III 15159. (© Florian Himmler)

**RIGHT**
Legionary horn-players on a metope of the Tropaeum Traiani. In battle, the standards were advanced according to the signals of the horns. (© C. Chirita)

According to Vegetius, the *tuba* 'calls the soldiers to battle, and sounds again for a retreat'. He also specifies that the *cornu* directed the movements of the standards. It therefore instigated movement in battle after the *tuba* had sounded the attack. In camp, the *tuba* was used to announce the watches, fatigues and drills (Vegetius 2.2). We would therefore expect every century to have possessed a *cornicen* and a *tubicen*.

If we follow Maurice (*Strategicon* 3.2) and place a horn player in the centre of the second rank of the century, he was well placed to receive instructions directly from the centurion. The use of the *cornu* required both hands. The gravestone of Aurelius Bitus, a *cornicen* of *legio II Adiutrix*, portrays him holding his instrument with both hands, while his small shield is suspended by his left arm. *Cornicines* must have found it difficult to defend themselves. Bitus' epitaph informs us that he was 'lost in war' (*CIL* III 15159).

The *cornicines* on Trajan's Column have similar small round shields. The legionaries around the vulnerable horn player must have been charged with keeping him alive. When Marius sent a total of five trumpeters and horn players on a special mission to confuse the enemy, he selected four centurions to act as their bodyguards (Sallust, *War With Jugurtha* 93.8).

## The number of ranks

We do not know how many ranks a legionary century formed in battle. Our evidence for the depth of battle lines is extremely limited. At Pharsalus in 48 BC, Pompey's battle lines were ten ranks deep (Frontinus, *Stratagems* 2.3.22–23). Josephus mentions security cordons, rather than actual battle lines, of infantry formed in three ranks, followed by three more of cavalry, and a rank of archers (*Jewish War* 2.173; 5.131). The *Strategicon* is insistent that in a field battle a line of less than four ranks was not strong enough (12.b.17).

In AD 67, Vespasian's legionaries marched into Judaea six abreast (Josephus, *Jewish War* 3.124). It has been suggested that the number of files in this marching column is indicative of the number of ranks in the battle line, because the column could wheel to form its line of battle (Goldsworthy 1996, 189). However, in marching order, the standards were clustered together ceremonially at the front of the column and, as a consequence, the standard bearers were not in a position to immediately lead their centuries into action (Josephus, *Jewish War* 3.123 and Arrian, *Battle Line Against the Alani* 3, 10). It is also worth noting that in AD 135 Arrian's legionaries marched four abreast, but formed a battle line of eight ranks (*ibid.* 4, 15–18).

Arrian's battle line suggests two possible deployments for the *centuria* of the Early Empire. First, keeping in mind that the first four ranks were armed with 'pikes' (probably *pila*), and the rear four ranks were armed with *lanceae* (light javelins), it is possible that the battle line was formed from two centuries, one formed up immediately behind the other, each in four ranks of 20. The second possibility is that the battle line was formed by centuries arrayed in eight ranks of ten men.

## Centurial titles and deployment

The manipular legion comprised 30 maniples: ten of *hastati* ('spearmen'), ten of *principes* ('best men') and ten of *triarii* ('third line men'). At the end of the 2nd century BC, the maniples of the legion were grouped into ten cohorts and the maniple was split into two centuries, so each cohort had two centuries of *hastati*, two of *principes*, and two of *pili*. *Pili* was another title for the *triarii*

Fragment of the epitaph of a career centurion, who served at least three legions and ended his career as a *hastatus prior*. *CIL* XIII 1839. (© R. Benoît)

(Varro, *On the Latin Language* 5.89). The maniples of the *triarii* were half the size of the other maniples, but there is no indication that the centuries of the *pili* in the cohortal legion were smaller than those of the *principes* or *hastati*.

The paired centuries were designated *prior* ('front' or 'first') and *posterior* ('rear' or 'following'). The title *posterior* suggests it formed up behind the *prior* century, but in his account of the Sabis (57 BC), where his army was in a makeshift *simplex acies* (single battle line), Caesar states that he ordered the 'maniples' to open up so the legionaries had room to wield their swords (*Gallic War* 2.25). As Polybius emphasizes, the legionary required considerable room in which to use his sword and shield effectively (18.30.7–8). If Caesar used 'maniple' to refer to paired centuries, it would follow that the *prior centuria* was originally the right half of Polybius' maniple, and the *posterior centuria* was the left half (6.24.8).

In the Middle Republic, the famous *triplex acies*, or triple battle line, was formed by maniples of *hastati* in the first line, *principes* in the second and *triarii* in the third. According to Caesar, the *triplex acies* of the Late Republican legion was formed by four cohorts in the first line, three in the second and three in the third (*Civil War* 1.83). As we have seen, Caesar may have used 'maniple' to indicate paired centuries, but more often he employed it as a generic term for infantry units (e.g. *Gallic War* 6.34, 40).

It seems probable that, despite retaining the old manipular titles (cf. the *princeps prior* of *Civil War* 3.64), the centuries making up Caesar's cohorts were deployed side-by-side. If they were deployed in three lines based on their manipular titles, there would be no point in forming a *triplex acies* of cohorts in a 4-3-3 arrangement. Varro, who fought against Caesar at Pharsalus in 48 BC, suggests that the manipular formations were not relevant in his day: 'these words [*hastatus, princeps, triarius*] were less perspicuous later when military matters had changed' (*On the Latin Language* 5.89; *contra* Speidel 2005, 290). Thus we often speak of the move from manipular to cohort tactics, but a better description may be the change from manipular to centurial tactics, because the cohort did not have a commanding officer.

## Command of the cohort

The legion is a rather curious military organization. The manipular legion did not have a commander (Isaac 1998, 389–90). The cohortal legion did, eventually, receive a commanding officer (*legatus*), but the institution of the rank probably had more to do with providing the friends and clients of Late Republican generals with lucrative posts than it did with military necessity. Caesar's legions sometimes received a legate only on the eve of battle and not necessarily for the purposes of command. In 58 BC, legates were appointed to act as witnesses to the *virtus* of legionaries (*Gallic War* 1.52).

The manipular legion, and the cohortal legion, had six tribunes, but they did not possess permanent tactical responsibilities (Isaac 1998, 399). If necessity required, legionary tribunes had the rank, class and authority to command complete battle lines in combat. The example of Publius Licinius Crassus is instructive. During the battle against Ariovistus (58 BC) 'Young Publius Crassus was in command of the cavalry... He could move more easily than those who were engaged in the fight and he sent the third line [of cohorts] to aid our struggling men [in the leading battle lines]. So the battle was restored and all of the enemy turned and fled, not ceasing in their flight until they reached the river Rhine, some five miles away.' (Caesar, *Gallic War* 1.52–53)

Crassus *did* have a definite tactical command, but his leadership of the cavalry was probably an ad hoc appointment which lasted only for the course of the battle; see above on the appointment of legionary legates before this battle. What should interest us here is how a member of Rome's ruling elite acted, and how predominantly plebeian centurions and legionaries accepted his authority and followed his order.

Legionary tribunes of the Early Empire could be allocated command over part of an army for the course of a battle (e.g. Arrian, *Battle Line Aainst the Alani* 24 – tribunes of *legio XII Fulminata* command the left wing), but such posts were temporary. Only the legate and the 60 centurions held permanent tactical commands. Who then filled the gap in the chain of command between the centurion and the legate? Why do we not hear of legionary cohort commanders?

The simple answer is that there were no legionary cohort commanders. This is very difficult for some to swallow because they erroneously conceive of the Roman army as being like a modern military organization. The cohort is viewed best as a grouping of cooperative centuries, as a legion in miniature. Like the manipular legion, the cohort did not require a commander because its constituent parts knew how to work together from training and prior experience (cf. Isaac 1998, 393). Caesar's battle narratives seem to be dominated by the manoeuvres of cohorts, but at closer inspection we find that Caesar writes about the relatively simple manoeuvres of battle lines composed of cohorts, and cohorts were built from centuries.

Successive generations of scholars, keen to fill the apparent gap in the legionary chain of command, have proposed that the leading centurion of the cohort, the *pilus prior*, acted as its commander. However, Professor Benjamin Isaac has comprehensively refuted such assertions (1998, 392–401). In the strict class system of ancient Rome, even senior centurions were mere *caligati* (boot-wearers) and could not command bodies of men larger in size than a century (cf. Gilliam 1946). Only men of equestrian and senatorial rank could command cohorts.

Other cohorts of the Imperial Roman army – auxiliary and Praetorian – *did* have commanders because, unlike Republican or Imperial legionary cohorts, they were distinct and independent units. Only when a legionary cohort was operating away from its parent legion did it become an independent formation (*vexillatio*). It would then receive a commander of suitably high rank, usually senatorial and later equestrian, and a standard (*vexillum*), to allow it to function independently.

It should be noted here that legionary vexillations were not necessarily formed by detaching cohorts alone. In AD 128, one cohort of the *legio III*

*Augusta* was on detached duty in the province of Proconsular Africa, while another substantial vexillation had been sent to reinforce a *legio III*, either *Gallica* or *Cyrenaica*. In his speech to the legion, Hadrian reveals that this detachment was formed by removing a cohort and four men from all the other centuries in the legion (*ILS* 2487; Speidel 2006, 8, reads 'you gave a cohort and five men from each *centuria* to the fellow Third Legion').

Returning to the question of command of the legionary cohort, Isaac notes that 'in the period of the principate, there was an element missing without which no modern army could function', namely there was an absence of legionary cohort commanders equivalent to modern battalion commanders, and a lack of standard bearers and trumpeters at battalion (= cohort) level to transmit orders. 'Yet the Roman army did function, perhaps because the decisions which had to be made in battle at lower levels were simpler than those made in modern warfare' (Isaac 1998, 401).

The seeming anomaly in the absence of 'middle tactical management' from the legion is explained by the limitations of communication on the battlefield. While the fighting was underway, the first, and sometimes even the second, battle line was beyond the control of the general and his lieutenants (cf. Caesar, *Gallic War* 1.52).

### A return to manipular tactics?

In AD 128, the emperor Hadrian observed the training exercises of *legio III Augusta* and auxiliary regiments at Lambaesis. The emperor's praise and criticisms of the manoeuvres were recorded, presumably by the legion's clerks, and inscribed on a monument in the legion's parade ground.

Speidel's recent interpretation of the surviving fragments of the inscription suggests that the emperor commended individually the *pili*, *principes* and *hastati* of the legion after they had completed a series of manoeuvres. Speidel asserts that the emperor was not only speaking to groups of centurions according to their rank (*pili* being the most senior and *hastati* the junior), but addressing them as officers of battle lines organized in the old manipular manner.

Also influenced by a small corpus of epigraphic centurial symbols, which might indicate the position of the legionary centurions, and consequently their centuries, in the battle line (see Mann 1997 for the problems of interpretation), Speidel proposes that the Imperial legions had abandoned the Caesarian *triplex acies* of cohorts in a 4-3-3 arrangement (not attested since the 40s BC), and returned to the formation of battle lines based on the centurions' titles (Speidel 2005; 2006, 28–41).

It should be emphasized that some of Speidel's restorations of the broken Lambaesis text are very tenuous, and previous scholars of Hadrian's speech have assumed the emperor was addressing groups of centurions by seniority and not according to their possible tactical functions and places in the battle lines. However, if Speidel's interpretation is correct, this would indicate that the legionaries fought in the manner of the Middle Republic, that is in distinct battle lines of *pili*, *principes* and *hastati*. Although Hadrian addressed the *pili* first on account of their seniority in the Early Imperial centurial hierarchy, and it is commonly assumed that they formed the front ranks of the legions, the battle order would be the 20 centuries of *hastati* in the first line, followed by the 20 centuries of *principes* in the second, and the 20 centuries of *pili* in the third (cf. Wheeler 2004, 165–66; adopted by Speidel 2005, 290).

The presence of *hastati*, *principes* and *pili* would mean that every cohort was essentially a legion in miniature. When detached from its parent unit it could 'snap-on' to the similarly organized vexillation, or even a complete legion, from the other side of the vast Empire. Standardized training and armament (perhaps with an emphasis on longer-range missiles for those in the rear ranks) meant that every legionary knew his place and function in the battle lines.

Titius Barbius Titianus, commissioned as a legionary centurion following 16 or 17 years' service in the Praetorian Guard, ended his career as the *centurio hastatus* of the first cohort of *legio II Traiana* (ILS 2652). If Speidel's interpretation of the Lambaesis inscription is correct, Titianus commanded the century at the honorific right of the first battle line in the *triplex acies* formation. Publius Turranius Severus, another centurion of the 2nd century AD, was the *hastatus prior* of the sixth cohort of *legio XV Apollinaris*, and later served as the *princeps posterior* of the fifth cohort of *legio IIII Flavia Felix* (AE 1988, 1044). Again, according to Speidel's interpretation, Severus commanded centuries in the first and second battle lines of the *triplex acies*.

In the *triplex acies*, the century of the *primus pilus* would have been positioned in the third and last battle line, but why then do we find *primi pili* in the front ranks in the two major battles of AD 69? At the second battle of Cremona, it is clear that the *primus pilus* of *legio VII Galbiana* was fighting in the front rank. At the first battle, *legio XXI Rapax* lost its eagle when its leading ranks were over-run by *I Adiutrix*. This indicates that the eagle-bearer was fighting at the front (Tacitus, *Histories* 3.22 and 2.43). (The *aquilifer* carried the standard of the legion and doubled as the *signifer* of the century of the *primus pilus*.) The simple solution is that legions were not bound to fight in the *triplex acies*. If *VII Galbiana* and *XXI Rapax* were arrayed in single battle lines (*simplex acies*, a formation sometimes adopted by Caesar's legions), their *primi pili* and eagle-bearers would have fought in the front rank.

However, we must be cautious. The *triplex acies* is not clearly attested in the frustratingly vague battle narratives of the 2nd century AD. In fact, the best account of a legionary battle formation comes from reign of Hadrian, and suggests something more akin to a Macedonian phalanx (Arrian, *Battle Line Against the Alani* 15–18 – most likely an atypical formation).

Aurelius Mucianus, a *lanciarius* of *legio II Parthica*, holding what may be a quiver of javelins. The inscription states that he belonged to the century of the *pilus posterior* of the ninth cohort. *AE* 1993, 1575. (© B. Gagnon)

# EQUIPMENT AND APPEARANCE

The essential panoply of the legionary was the *pilum*, *gladius* and *scutum*, helmet (*galea* or *cassis*) and some form of body armour (*lorica*) (Bishop & Coulston 2006; Robinson 1975).

## Pilum

The *pilum* was the defining weapon of the Roman legionary (Livy 9.19.7). As a close range missile it was deadly, 'breaking down all before it' (Tibullus 3.7.90). As a throwing weapon, it was designed to punch through shield and armour (Livy 10.39.12), but it was also used for thrusting (cf. Appian, *Civil Wars* 2.76, Plutarch *Antony* 45.3; Tacitus, *Histories* 4.29). Metope 35 of the Tropaeum Traiani at Adamclisi shows a legionary dispatching a *falx*-wielding Dacian warrior with a downwards thrust of his heavy *pilum*.

 **WEAPONS**

Swords and dagger. The legionary sword was a cut-and-thrust weapon. The short Pompeii-type *gladius* from Newstead (**1**), dating to the end of the 1st century AD, is restored here with a bone hilt assembly of typical shape. The broken sword from Hod Hill (**2**) was probably a medium-length weapon (mid-to-later 1st century AD), and is restored here with a relatively long blade. In the second half of our period, ring-pommel swords became popular. The example here (**3**) is a based on the short sword from Pevensey (late 2nd century AD). The large dagger (**4**), based on the blade from Tuuchyna and hilt plate from Bar Hill, is typical of the type in use towards the end of our period.

Missile weapons. The principal javelin of the legionary was the *pilum*; (**5**) demonstrates the method of attaching a flat-tanged *pilum* shank to a wooden shaft. The legionary used other missile weapons with a variety of heads. The examples here, based on finds from Newstead and other Roman forts in Flavian and Antonine Scotland, range from leaf-shaped spear and lance heads (**6–8**), to javelins with pyramidal armour-piercing points (**9**), and barbed heads (**10**).

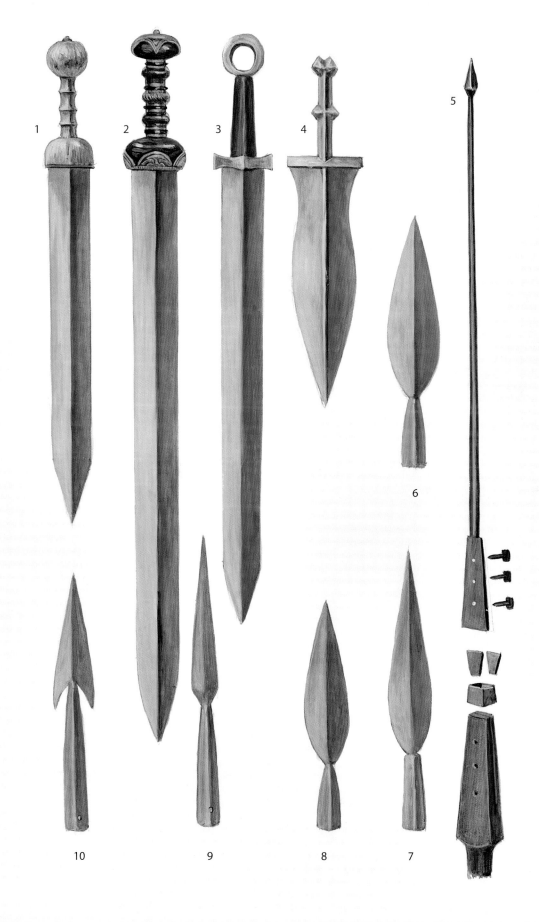

By the end of the 2nd century AD, the *pilum* appears to have become something of a specialist weapon, but it remained in general use throughout our period. Castricius Victor is depicted on his gravestone holding two *pila*: a heavy flat-tanged *pilum*, and a lighter socketed *pilum*. Flat-tanged *pila* are also shown on the gravestone of Valerius Crispus and the Croy Hill relief. Some of the Adamclisi metopes show *pila* with what appear to be round or oval metal weights (there are no archaeological finds to confirm this). Such weighted *pila* are also known from the gravestones of imperial guardsmen, but do not feature on legionary memorials.

A narrow *pilum* point and a collet (used to secure the metal shank to the wooden shaft of the javelin) from Newstead. In the National Museum of Scotland. (© RHC Archive)

Unusually large *pila* heads from Bar Hill on the Antonine Wall. In the Hunterian Museum, Glasgow. (© RHC Archive)

### Lancea

The *pilum* may have been the defining weapon of the legionary, but it was not his only shafted weapon. In our period, some legionaries specialized in the use of the *lancea* (cf. Tacitus, *Histories* 1.79). These men were known as *lanciarii* (Tomlin 1999, 133; *AE* 1998, 839a), but the title did not achieve official recognition until the early 3rd century AD (*IRL* 24–27).

The *lancea* (or *lancia*) is primarily thought of as a throwing weapon but, like the *pilum*, it was also used for thrusting, and it came in a variety of forms and sizes. Some *lanceae* were light and slim javelins. The smallest type appears to have been called the *minor subarmalis* ('small, under the arm'), as spare *lanceae* could easily be tucked under the arm or grasped behind the shield (Tomlin 1999, 133–37).

A cavalryman of *legio II Augusta* on the Bridgeness distance slab rides down the enemy. He may be armed with what soldiers called the *lancea pugnatoria*, the heavy fighting lance. *RIB* I 2139. (© RHC Archive)

The *minor subarmalis* may be depicted on a relief sculpture on a column base from the legionary headquarters building at Mainz. It depicts a soldier, presumably a legionary, running with three short javelins, one ready in his right hand, two others held behind his oval shield. The weapons are only slightly longer than the shield itself, but the area available on the column base may have determined the size. The relief dates to the later 1st century AD (*RL* 26).

The soldier's running pose suggests that he was a skirmisher, perhaps similar to the *velites* ('swift-ones') of the Republican legions. The gravestone of Flavoleius Cordus, a legionary of *legio XIV Gemina*, who died before AD 43, shows him with a large oval shield and a single javelin with a throwing thong (*amentum*) to help extend its range (*RL* 31). The javelin is probably a type of *lancea*, as Isidore of Seville tells us 'a *lancea* is a spear with an *amentum* in the middle [of the shaft]' (*Etymologies* 18.7.5–6). This weapon is longer than the javelins held by the soldier on the Mainz relief.

Pompeii-type *gladius* from Newstead. This variety of sword is named after examples lost in Pompeii during the eruption of Vesuvius in AD 79. In the National Museum of Scotland. (© RHC Archive)

Other *lanceae* were more substantial and used by cavalry as thrusting weapons. This type may have been called the *lancea pugnatoria*, the 'fighting lance' (Tomlin 1999). Such a weapon is recorded on a report of the *ala Sebosiana*, dating to the end of the 1st century AD. It may be that the long 'spear' often depicted on the funerary monuments of Roman cavalry, where the trooper is shown trampling a barbarian and stabbing down at him, is the *lancea pugnatoria*.

In the defence of their camp at Cremona, Vitellian legionaries used *lanceae* and pikes (*conti*) to prise apart the shields of Flavian legionaries in *testudo* formation (Tacitus, *Histories* 3.27). Perhaps these *lanceae* were particularly hefty examples of the weapon, but we should also consider that Tacitus was using the word as a generic term for a shafted weapon.

Thus *lancea* described a wide range of weapons. We must assume that *lanceae* were distinguishable from *hastae* (spears) by some particular feature, and like *pila* came in a wide range of light and heavy, and socketed and tanged versions, but that all were recognizable as part of the same family by the long metal shank between the head of the weapon and the wooden shaft. The *amentum* was a characteristic of some *lanceae*, but not all lances had the throwing thong, so there was presumably some other feature of shafts or iron heads that identified them as *lanceae*.

## Swords and daggers

The main sword of the legionary, at least in the first half of our period, was the Pompeii-type *gladius*, so-called after finds of this particular pattern lost at Pompeii during the eruption of Vesuvius in AD 79. Contrary to popular belief, *gladius* does not mean short sword; it simply means 'sword'. However, the Pompeii-type *gladius* was a genuine short sword. Its blade, with parallel edges and a triangular point, ranged from 42 to 55cm in length. By the 2nd century AD, another sword was becoming favoured by some legionaries. It was also

 **D**

**RECENT RECRUIT OF *LEGIO VII GALBIANA*, AD 69**

Hastily enrolled by conscription (*dilectus*) in Spain in AD 68, this young legionary of *VII Hispana* (better known as *Galbiana*), is depicted in a mixture of old and new equipment. Old equipment was certainly stockpiled for use as spares or to equip troops in emergencies.

This legionary is protected by a *scutum* (shield) with curved sides, and a mail shirt with shoulder-doubling, both typical of the legions of Augustus (27 BC – AD 14). However, a swordsman depicted on a column base at Mainz appears to have a *scutum* with curved sides (*RL* 31, later 1st century AD), and a soldier of Trajan (AD 98–117) wears a mail shirt with shoulder-doubling on one of the Ephesus ivories. In order to absorb the shock of blows, our legionary wears his mail over a padded garment, perhaps known as a *subarmalis* ('under the armour'). The lightning bolt device on the shield follows a pattern on Trajan's Column.

The legionary's *pilum* (heavy javelin) is of a type unchanged since the late 1st century BC, except for the addition of a metal weight. His bronze helmet (Robinson's Imperial Italic type C, after an example lost near Cremona, probably in AD 69) and Pompeii *gladius* are of the latest type. At the end of the century, his *caligae*, the classic heavy sandals of the legionary, would be replaced by fully enclosed boots.

The inserts show a diagram of a *lorica segmentata* cuirass (**1**) (Robinson's Corbridge type A), and an iron helmet (**2**) (Robinson's Imperial Gallic type H), both in use in the later 1st century AD, but perhaps not as widespread as the depiction of the former on Trajan's Column, and the popularity of the latter with modern re-enactors, might suggest. While on campaign, the legionary carried personal belongings and rations in a leather satchel (**3**) (*loculus*), drank from a robust iron flask (**4**) (based on an example from Newstead), dug the ditches of his camp with a military pickaxe (**5**) (*dolabra*), and cut the sods which formed the ramparts with a turf-cutter (**6**).

Ring-pommel sword from Pevensey (top) and the broken sword from Hod Hill (below), which probably had a medium-length blade. The wooden sword (or dagger, bottom) may be a practice weapon. In the British Museum. (© Steven D. P. Richardson)

Detail of the distinctive hilt of the short ring-pommel sword from Pevensey. Ring-pommel swords were adopted from Rome's trans-Danubian enemies. In the British Museum. (© Steven D. P. Richardson)

Detail of the hilt assembly of the Hod Hill sword, the decoration of which shows native British influences. (© Steven D. P. Richardson)

short-bladed but had a distinctive ring-pommel hilt, and was probably adopted from the Sarmatians and Rome's other trans-Danubian enemies.

Caesar's legionaries fought with a medium-length cut-and-thrust sword, and not all of the legionaries of our period were satisfied with short Pompeii-type and ring-pommel swords. The blade of the *gladius* from Hod Hill is broken, but it probably had a notably long blade. Towards the close our period, more legionaries were probably using longer swords, and by the 3rd century AD *spathae* ('long swords') were the norm. However, the term 'long sword' is misleading. Roman *spathae* were not long by medieval or early modern standards. *Spathae* (better, *gladii*, the term used by Roman soldiers like Ammianus; *spatha* is usually imposed on weapons by modern scholars influenced by Vegetius) were medium-length weapons, suitable for cutting and thrusting. The fact that swords became somewhat longer does not mean that the Roman legionary fought in a markedly different manner.

In the 2nd century AD, the traditional four-ring method of suspending the scabbard from the baldric was gradually replaced by the slide. The scabbard slide was probably another adoption from Rome's trans-Danubian enemies. The scabbard of the dagger (*pugio*) continued to use the traditional method of suspension. During our period, daggers became larger, some with blades in excess of 30cm. In the late 1st century BC, and early 1st century AD, legionaries had lavished their pay on elaborately decorated dagger scabbards, but by end of our period the scabbard was a plain iron frame with insert panels.

The *pugio* was useful weapon, especially in close combat. During the siege of Vetera (AD 69–70), the legionaries of *XV Primigenia* and *V Alaudae* defended the ramparts with *pila*, shield bosses and *pugiones*: 'They beat them [Civilis' Batavians and Germans] down with the bosses of their shields, and followed this action with their *pila*. Many who scaled the walls, they stabbed with daggers.' (Tacitus, *Histories* 4.29)

A typical dagger and highly decorated scabbard of the 1st century AD from Carnuntum. In the 2nd century, legionaries used a larger dagger housed in a plain scabbard. (© Florian Himmler)

## Shield

The legionary employed two main types of shield: the curved rectangular *scutum* and a flat oval shield. The scutum is considered the classic shield of the legionary because of its familiarity from Trajan's Column, as well as depictions on the Adamclisi metopes, the column base reliefs from the legionary headquarters building at Mainz (*RL* 31–32), and the gravestone of Valerius Crispus of *legio VIII Augusta*.

By the early 3rd century AD, the *scutum* had been superseded by the oval shield. It is not clear why, for the *scutum*, in its various forms, had proved useful in close and open order fighting in various terrains. That the *scutum* was still the principal shield of the legionary at the end of our period is demonstrated by the relief of three legionaries (probably cut from a gravestone) from Croy Hill on the Antonine Wall (*c*.AD 142–161), and by the votive stele of Ares. The latter served in *legio II Traiana* and was recruited in *c*.AD 162. At the end of his service (*c*.AD 188), he dedicated to his namesake, the war god Ares, his helmet, sword and *scutum* (*IRL* 43; Stoll 2005).

As noted above, the flat oval shield is depicted on one of the Mainz column bases, used by a light-armed legionary (*RL* 26), but it was also carried by regular legionaries, like Castricius Victor. His shield has a thunderbolt blazon of the type well known from Trajan's Column. An incident in the second battle of Cremona suggests that each unit had a distinctive blazon: 'Two men of Vespasian's party wrought a notable achievement. Their side was being severely damaged by a ballista, and these two, seizing shields from among the spoils of the Vitellian faction, mingled with the opposing ranks, and made their way to the engine just as if they belonged to that side. Thus they managed to cut the ropes of the engine, so that not another missile could be discharged from it.' (Dio 65.14.2; cp. Tacitus, *Histories* 3.23)

Hilt plate of a dagger from Bar Hill on the Antonine Wall. The dagger of the Antonine era was a substantial weapon with a blade of *c*.30cm. In the Hunterian Museum. (© RHC Archive)

Decorated boss from the *scutum* of Iunius Dubitatus of *legio VIII Augusta*. It was discovered in the River Tyne, where it may have been deposited as a votive offering. (© RHC Archive)

Detail of Castricius Victor's oval shield, with its classic lightning bolt blazon. The boss appears to be decorated with a face. (© Florian Himmler)

To help identify individual legionaries at the first battle of Tapae (AD 88), the general Tettius Iulianus ordered 'that the soldiers should inscribe their own names as well as those of their centurions upon their shields, in order that those of their number who should perform any particularly good or base deed might be more readily recognized' (Dio 67.10.1).

The shield was really part of the Roman warrior's offensive panoply. It was used to barge and batter (Tacitus, *Histories* 2.42, 4.29), and the *umbo* (shield boss) could be punched into an opponent's face (cf. Tacitus, *Agricola* 36.)

## Armour

Three main types of body armour (*lorica*) were used by legionaries in our period: articulated iron plate, iron mail, and scale of iron or bronze. The most famous Roman armour is, of course, *lorica segmentata*, the modern name for the cuirass of articulated iron plates. Its use was not as total as Trajan's Column suggests. It is not depicted on the Adamclisi metopes, nor on any gravestone bearing a portrait of a legionary, but the shoulder guard of a cuirass is perhaps to be seen on one of the Mainz column bases (*RL* 32).

The funerary monuments of Valerius Crispus and Castricius Victor show the deceased wearing mail shirts. The shirt of the former has a double layer of mail at the shoulders. The Adamclisi metopes show legionaries in long shirts of either mail or scale. The shirts are worn over arming garments, presumably padded to absorb the shock of blows, with layers of pteruges, fabric strips to protect the upper arms and thighs.

The Adamclisi legionaries have articulated arm guards (*manicae*) on their right arms. Finds of this armour are known from Newstead, Carlisle and Leon. They also wear full-length greaves, which cover the knees, but another type of greave used in our period was little more than a shin guard.

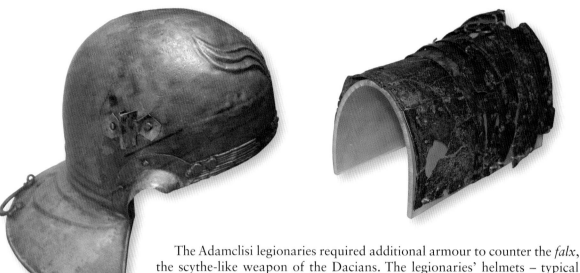

The Adamclisi legionaries required additional armour to counter the *falx*, the scythe-like weapon of the Dacians. The legionaries' helmets – typical Imperial Gallic or Italic types with broad neck guards and large cheek pieces – are reinforced with cross-braces. Towards the end of our period, legionaries started to use helmets of Robinson's Auxiliary Infantry and Cavalry types. These helmets offered substantial protection, leaving only a small t-shaped opening for the face. Such a helmet can be seen on the stele of Ares of *II Traiana* (*IRL* 43).

### Appearance

In our period, the legionary's basic clothing was a tunic, either sleeveless or long-sleeved, and belted at the waist by the *balteus* or *cingulum*. This was covered with decorative metal plates and worn in conjunction with an 'apron' of studded straps. Short trousers called *bracae* became the norm, and enclosed boots replaced *caligae*-type sandals. The standard cloak of the period was the heavy *paenula* (Sumner 2009).

Legionaries copied the fashion of the emperor, their fellow-soldier and commander-in-chief. From the Year of the Four Emperors (AD 69) to the death of Trajan (AD 117), legionaries generally wore their hair short and were clean shaven. Hadrian, the successor of Trajan, was a Hellenophile, and the soldiers copied his bushy hair and full beard.

## ON CAMPAIGN

Campaigns ranged from minor policing actions to wars of conquest. Trajan's Column depicts the latter, but presents a somewhat misleading view of the legionary on campaign.

### The evidence of Trajan's Column

Trajan's Column portrays the Dacian Wars of AD 101–102 and 105–106 in a great spiral frieze. It is dominated by two themes: auxiliary soldiers in combat, and legionary soldiers mostly engaged in construction and logistical work. This would appear to support the assertion of some that, even before Trajan became emperor (AD 98), legionaries had been relegated to a supporting role in battle. The example used to support this theory is the battle of Mons Graupius (AD 83), where the great victory over the Caledonians belonged exclusively to the auxiliary cohorts and *alae* (cavalry units) (Tacitus, *Agricola* 35–37).

**LEFT**
An Imperial Gallic helmet in Dorestad Museum made, unusually, of bronze. Note the plume holder above the ear guard, and the carry handle on the neck guard. (© mararie)

**RIGHT**
Section of a *manica*, an articulated arm guard, from Newstead. In the National Museum of Scotland. (© RHC Archive)

*Disciplina* and *labor*, discipline and hard work, are exemplified by legionaries on Trajan's Column. Identified by their *scuta* and *lorica segmentata*, Trajan's legionaries march to the war zone in impressive order and following a pep-talk (*adlocutio*) by the emperor, are soon put to work. They construct camps and fortifications, clear woods and prepare the felled timber, and build roads and bridges (Cichorius 1900, scenes 10, 11, 13, 15 and 18). The *dolabra*, the military pickaxe, is very much in evidence, bringing to mind the famous maxim of Corbulo about 'the *dolabra* being the weapon with which to beat the enemy' (Frontinus, *Stratagems* 4.7.2).

The legionaries are soon advancing towards the first major encounter with Decebalus' Dacian warriors, but they do so as pioneers, cutting a path through a forest for the rest of the army (Cichorius scenes 22–23; cf. Josephus, *Jewish War* 3.117–18). In the ensuing battle, which seems to represent the second battle of Tapae in AD 101/2 (Dio 68.8), the legionaries, and similarly equipped Praetorian Guardsmen, hold back, acting as a reserve (Cichorius scenes 23–24). Like the legionaries at the battle of Mons Graupius in AD 83, they are not required to fight (Tacitus, *Agricola* 35–37). The regular auxiliary troops, and a bare-chested irregular armed with a club, have more than enough *virtus* to defeat the Dacians.

As the campaign continues to wind its way up the Column, some auxiliaries are reduced to garrison duty, but find themselves fighting off Dacians equipped with a battering ram, and a few experience a taste of the *labor* of the legionaries, helping to load and unload transport ships (Cichorius scenes 32–35). We soon return to action and, again, the auxiliaries and the bare-chested irregulars are at the forefront in fights against Sarmatian cataphracts. Contrast an engagement in AD 69, where legionaries of *III Gallica* defeated the Sarmatian Rhoxolani:

The so-called Camomile Street soldier, resplendent in his *paenula*, the all-weather cloak of the legionary. An ornately decorated apron hangs from his belt. In the Museum of London. (© D. B. Campbell)

Entrenching and pioneer tools from the Antonine Wall. The *dolabra* (top left) and axe also functioned as useful weapons in battle. In the Hunterian Museum. (© RHC Archive)

Legionaries fell trees and build a road on Trajan's Column (scene 56). Two severed heads, perhaps trophies taken by the legionaries, are impaled on stakes beside the new road. (Cichorius 1900, plate 40)

The Roman soldier in his cuirass moved readily about, attacking the enemy with his *pilum*, which he threw, or with his *lanceae*. When the situation required he used his short sword and cut down the helpless Sarmatians at close quarters, for they do not use the shield for defensive purposes. Finally the few who escaped the battle hid themselves in the swamps, where they lost their lives from the cruel winter or the severity of their wounds.

Tacitus, *Histories* 1.79

In the next major battle scene on Trajan's Column, the so-called night battle, a solitary legionary makes an appearance. In the following scene, legionaries are back to what appears to be their main task in this war: building forts and digging defensive ditches (Cichorius scenes 37–39).

Another battle follows (Cichorius scenes 40–41), a very large-scale affair, and the legionaries are not relegated to the sidelines. They fight alongside the auxiliaries and the bare-chested warriors. One legionary has his wounds attended to in what appears to be a field hospital, while others bring up catapults mounted on carts to 'fire' upon the enemy (for the use of legionary artillery in battle, see Tacitus, *Histories* 3.23 and Dio 65.14.2). The legionaries fight the Dacians at close quarters, and are clearly the equals of the auxiliaries in hand-to-hand combat.

 **FIGHTING STYLES**

The Roman legionary was not merely a swordsman; he was a sword-and-shield man. The *scutum*, used to block, guard and strike, was as essential to his fighting technique as the *gladius*. Here we see four legionaries (**1–4**), heavily armoured with cross-bracing on their helmets, *manica* arm guards and greaves, battling Dacian warriors armed with the scythe-like *falx*. The metopes on the Tropaeum Traiani at Adamclisi, which commemorate the Dacian Wars of the early 2nd century AD, indicate that a legionary fought with his left leg leading and the *scutum* held close to his body, from where it could be punched forwards, or raised up sharply to catch an opponent with its metal-edged rim (**2**). The metopes show the classic use of the sword in the under-arm thrust (**2, 3**), but also reveal over-arm cuts (**1**; the Roman sword was, after all, a cut-and-thrust weapon), and show that the grip on the sword could be reversed to add force to downward thrusts (**4**).

While a legionary *testudo* advances on the wall of a Dacian fortress, auxiliaries present to Trajan the heads they have taken in combat. Trajan's Column scenes 71–71. (Cichorius 1900, plate 51)

Following their brush with glory, the legionaries are quickly put back to work. A lucky few escape hard *labor* by guarding important Dacian prisoners of war, but the majority sweat in the building of forts, clearing of trees and construction of roads (Cichorius scenes 43, 51, 55, 56, 60).

The road-building scene (56), however, has a notable element. Just behind the toiling legionaries, the heads of two Dacians are impaled on stakes. What are we to make of this? Is this a reference to legionary *virtus*, the heads being trophies taken by the legionaries in an action that secured the area? It is impossible to know. When auxiliaries take heads on the Column, there is no ambiguity (e.g. Cichorius scenes 24, 72). In one striking scene (Cichorius 113), auxiliaries and legionaries assault the walls of Sarmizegethusa (probably the siege of AD 106). Having reached the top of the ladder – no mean feat in itself – an auxiliary proceeds to decapitate one of the Dacian defenders. As in the battle of Tapae scene (Cichorius 24), an auxiliary, rather than a citizen legionary or Praetorian, is the exemplar of Roman *virtus*.

# BATTLE

### Siege warfare

Legionaries perform mundane but essential tasks on the Column. As well as construction work, they gather forage (Cichorius scene 110; the apparent looting in scene 124 may actually depict legionary quartermasters gathering up abandoned enemy supplies) and build boats (133), presumably to function as troop or supply transports. They steadfastly defend their forts, sometimes fighting invaders in the annexes, or protect the walls with their trusty pickaxes (96). At other times their aggression is proactive. In Cichorius' scene 62, they appear to be fighting their way into mountainous terrain and targeting

Legionaries, exposed to attack from above, use picks to demolish the fortifications of Sarmizegethusa. To the right, a mixed group of auxiliaries and legionaries provide 'covering fire' and attempt to use their shields to shelter the demolition squad. Trajan's Column scene 117. (Cichorius 1900, plate 87)

Dacian villages. As we have seen, legionaries do fight in open battle (add Cichorius scenes 72 – coming up from the reserve – and 115), but the Column tends to suggest that auxiliaries are the battle winners, while legionaries are the ultimate support troops and excel at consolidation of conquests.

On the other hand, the legionaries do excel in siege warfare and can be seen constructing siege works and artillery positions (e.g. Cichorius scenes 65, 66, 117). Legionaries act as assault troops (with auxiliaries at 115, 117), and in one scene (71), we witness the acme of legionary *disciplina*: the *testudo*. The legionaries have to walk over the bodies of the fallen as they advance on the enemy wall, but they still maintain the walls and roof of the shield formation (hence the name 'tortoise'). In another scene (Cichorius 117), legionaries use their picks to demolish the defences of Sarmizegethusa. This scene represents another pinnacle of *disciplina* with a large dose of *virtus*. Despite being unable to defend themselves from enemy missiles, the stoic legionaries hack at the walls and prise away blocks.

## Furious fighters

It is easy to overemphasize the example of Mons Graupius and the avoidance of spilling Roman blood, or more precisely citizen blood, by leaving the fighting to the non-citizen auxiliaries (Tacitus, *Agricola* 35). A brief examination of the sources for the battles of AD 68–70 demonstrates that legionaries were aggressive fighters, sometimes uncontrollably so. At Vesontio (AD 68), the legionaries acted without orders when they attacked and annihilated Vindex's army (Dio 63.24.3–4). Two years later, during the siege of Jerusalem, legionaries ignored the vocal and visual orders of their commander, the future emperor Titus, and deliberately set fire to the Temple. Josephus, the Jewish rebel commander and historian, describes the Romans as being beyond control: 'neither persuasion nor threats could restrain their violence' (*Jewish War* 6.257–58). At the battles of Cremona in AD 69, legionaries were always in the front ranks and they fought madly (emphasized by Dio 65.12.2–3).

Bronze plate from a catapult belonging to *legio IV Macedonica* (a Vitellian legion), and lost in the fighting at Cremona in AD 69. Tacitus and Dio remark on the Vitellians' use of artillery in the second battle, and how it inflicted serious casualties on the Flavian army. (*Notizie degli Scavi* 1887, tav. 4)

At the battle of Vetera in AD 70, auxiliary regiments formed the leading battle line of the Roman army against Civilis' Germans. When the auxiliaries were pushed back, the legions, coming up from the second battle line, 'took up the contest, checked the fury of the enemy, and the battle again became equal' (Tacitus, *Histories* 5.18). The battle was eventually won by a combination of an outflanking manoeuvre performed by the auxiliary cavalry, and a frontal assault by the legions against the main German battle line.

On Trajan's Column, the *virtus* of legionaries is not completely ignored, but it is certainly downplayed, probably for the sake of thematic balance. The *disciplina* of the legionaries is complemented by the *virtus* of the auxiliaries (who were in fact capable of engineering work, e.g. Tacitus, *Histories* 3.6), and together they prove an irresistible combination. That legionaries still were exemplars of *virtus* in Trajan's wars is confirmed by the 'metopes' (relief panels) of the Tropaeum Traiani ('Trajan's Trophy') at Adamclisi in Romania. This huge victory monument was erected by the army of the province of Moesia to celebrate its bloody victories over the Dacians and their allies.

**LEGIONARY VERSUS LEGIONARY AT THE FIRST BATTLE OF CREMONA, AD 69**

In mid-April AD 69, the armies of Vitellius and Otho clashed near Cremona. The large size of the armies, coupled with the varied nature of the terrain, meant that some fought in extended battle order on open ground by the River Po (e.g. the Vitellian *XXI Rapax* and the Othonian *I Adiutrix*), while others had to contend with the obstacles of vineyards and orchards of fruit trees, as illustrated here. According to Tacitus, the legionaries in the vineyards could not maintain regular order and fought as individuals or in small groups. In another sector of the battlefield, legionaries fought on the raised platform of the Postumian Way. 'They struggled at close quarters, pressing the weight of their bodies behind their shields. They did not throw *pila*, but crashed swords and axes [i.e. those normally used for pioneer work] through helmets and armour' (Tacitus, *Histories* 2.42; cf. *Annals* 3.46 for the use of entrenching tools in battle). Victory eventually fell to the Vitellian legionaries, who outnumbered the Othonians and entered the battle in better order.

The Trophy does not ignore auxiliaries, but it tends to emphasize the role of legionary infantrymen. Heavily armoured in long shirts of mail or scale, and with additional limb protection (articulated arm guards and greaves) necessary for men who fought at the closest of quarters (e.g. metopes 17–23), the legionaries fight as swordsmen and occasionally as spearmen (e.g. metope 31). In metope 35, a legionary uses his *pilum* as a thrusting weapon. The legionaries dispatch their warrior opponents in often brutal fashion (metope 21, with mutilated corpses visible in metope 24). Women and children are terrorized and massacred (metopes 35 and 37). Despite the fury evident in these sculptures, *disciplina* is not absent from the Trophy. It is represented by important tactical control figures: standard-bearers, horn-players and centurions (e.g. metopes 41, 42 and 27).

The legionaries of Julius Caesar are usually held up as the classic exemplars of Roman *virtus*, but the victors of the battles of the Sabis and Pharsalus were the same men who bridged the Rhine and enveloped Alesia in complex siegeworks (Caesar, *Gallic War* 4.17–18; 7.72–74). The Caesarian legionary therefore exemplified *disciplina* as well as *virtus*, but the latter quality could sometimes overwhelm the former and lead to disaster, as occurred at Gergovia in 52 bc (*ibid.* 7.46–51).

While legionaries are usually depicted in the background of, or as a minority in, battle and siege scenes on Trajan's Column, they are at the forefront of the fighting on the metopes of the Tropaeum Traiani at Adamclisi. The only *labor* on the Trophy's metopes is brutal and – to the Romans – glorious combat. If we combine the predominant legionary themes on these two monuments, that is *disciplina* for the Column and *virtus* for the Trophy, we must arrive at the conclusion that the Trajanic legionary was very much like his Caesarian predecessor.

## Heroes

The literary sources for Trajan's Dacian Wars are poor, hence the focus on the scenes on Trajan's Column and Adamclisi metopes, but a number of inscriptions identify legionary heroes of the Wars. The centurions Aconius Statura, Claudius Vitalis and Aemilius Paternus all won a *corona vallaris* (rampart crown) for being the first to fight their way into an enemy camp (*CIL* XI 5992; *ILS* 2656, 2661). Their centuries would have been close behind, the legionaries motivated by the displays of aggressive *virtus*. The rampart conquered by Julius Rufus, a career centurion, must have been particularly heavily defended, for Trajan not only decorated him with a crown, but gave him the right to parade in a 'white uniform' (*AE* 1998, 1435).

Hadrian, the future emperor, served on Trajan's staff during the First Dacian War, and commanded *legio I Minervia* in the second war. According to the Historia Augusta, 'his many remarkable deeds won great renown' (*Hadrian* 3.6), and he was twice decorated (*CIL* III 550).

## AFTER THE BATTLE

Following a victory in a pitched battle, or a siege, legionaries would clap and cheer and raise the paean, the song of triumph (Josephus, *Jewish War* 6.403; cf. Herodian 3.7.3). In the 1st century BC, legionaries would also drum weapons against their shields (e.g. Appian, *Civil Wars* 5.37), and the practice may have continued into the 1st century AD (Cowan 2007). A trophy of captured arms might be erected (Tacitus, *Annals* 2.18), and standards were planted to proclaim Roman possession of conquered ground (Josephus, *Jewish War* 6.403). A sacrifice might be performed and the commander –

so long as he was a member of the imperial family – be acclaimed *imperator* (victorious commander). Following the capture of the Temple at Jerusalem in AD 70 'The Romans carried their standards into the temple courtyard and, setting them up opposite the eastern gate, there sacrificed to them [i.e. to the *genii* of the legions and centuries], and with rousing acclamations hailed Titus as *imperator*.' (Josephus, *Jewish War* 6.316).

Legionaries looted dead and dying opponents of valuables (Tacitus, *Histories* 3.25). Some took gruesome trophies. It is clear that Roman auxiliaries were head-hunters (see above), and recent research on the Babylonian Talmud suggests that during the Bar Kochba revolt (AD 132–135), legionaries covered their helmets with scalps taken from slaughtered Jewish rebels (Stiebel 2005; cp. Silius Italicus, *Punica* 5.131–39 for the practice in the 3rd century BC).

**H    THE CAMP OF THE NINTH LEGION ATTACKED BY THE CALEDONIANS, AD 82**

In AD 82, during Julius Agricola's penultimate season of campaigning in what is now Scotland, the Caledonian tribes launched a surprise night attack on the marching camp of *legio VIIII Hispana*. The battle site has been identified with various Roman camps, including Dalginross in Strathearn, and Fendoch at the mouth of the Sma' Glen. The Caledonians knew the legion was not at full strength; a *vexillatio* (detachment) was serving in Domitian's Chattan operations. On learning of the attack, Agricola brought up a relief force. The Caledonians found themselves trapped between two forces, and there was desperate fighting, especially in one of the gateways of the camp. The Romans eventually prevailed, but the proud legionaries of the Ninth denied that they had needed rescuing (Tacitus, *Histories* 26).

The reconstruction here is influenced by Tacitus' description of a similar attack on the camp of Petillius Cerialis in AD 70. Although surprised at night by Civilis' Germans, the bulk of Cerialis' men seem not to have panicked and, instead of scrabbling around in the dark for their shields and other armour, improvised defences with their clothes and fought the Germans as best they could (Tacitus, *Histories*, 5.22; and note *Annals* 3.46, and *Histories* 2.42, 3.27, for the use of entrenching tools in combat).

A relief panel of the Bridgeness distance slab (*RIB* I 2139) depicts the legate of *legio II Augusta* conducting a *suovetaurilia* sacrifice, probably as part of a religious ceremony to mark the completion of the Antonine Wall in AD 142. In the National Museum of Scotland. (© RHC Archive)

In the civil wars of AD 69, defeated legionaries were sometimes insulted and threatened with violence and even executed (Tacitus, *Histories* 3.31, 4.1), but when the fury of combat had waned, they were treated moderately and sometimes allowed to keep their standards and weapons (*ibid*. 3.31, 63, 4.2). Such was the fraternity between soldiers. Civilians, however, were raped, tortured for amusement, and taken as slaves (*ibid*. 2.56, 3.32–33; Dio 65.15). When Antonius Primus announced that captives taken during the sack of Cremona could not be sold as slaves, they were murdered by infuriated Flavian legionaries (Tacitus, *Histories* 3.34).

It was the duty of commanders of officers to witness and record brave deeds. Following the capture and demolition of Jerusalem in AD 70, Titus paraded his victorious army:

> Titus gave orders to the appointed officers to read out the names of all who had performed any brilliant feat during the war. Calling each up by name, he applauded them as they came forward, no less exultant over their exploits than if they were his own. He then placed crowns of gold upon their heads, presented them with golden torques, little golden spears (*hastae*) and standards made of silver (*vexilla*), and promoted each man to a higher rank. He further assigned to them out of the spoils silver and gold and garments and other booty in abundance. When all had been awarded as he judged each to have deserved, after invoking blessings on the whole army, he descended [from his tribunal] amidst many acclamations and proceeded to offer sacrifices of thanksgiving for his victory.
> Josephus, *Jewish War* 7.13–16

It was probably in this ceremony that Pellartius Celer, *armidoctor* of *legio XV Apollinaris*, was presented with his gold crown (*AE 1952, 153*).

# FURTHER READING

## Websites

Most of the inscriptions referred to above (*AE*, *CIL*, *ILS*, *IMS*, *RIB*, *Tit. Aq.*), and links to photographs of many, can be consulted on the Epigraphik-Datenbank Clauss/Slaby:

http://oracle-vm.ku-eichstaett.de:8888/epigr/epigraphik_en

Roman Army Talk is the best forum for discussion of the legions and all other Ancient military matters:

http://www.romanarmytalk.com

## References

BGU = *Berliner Griechische Urkunden*

Birley, E. B., 'A Note on the Title "Gemina"', *Journal of Roman Studies* 18 (1928), 56–60

Bishop, M. C., and Coulston, J. C. N., *Roman Military Equipment: From the Punic Wars to the Fall of Rome*, second edition, Oxford: 2006

Campbell, D. B., 'The Fate of the Ninth: The Curious Disappearance of Legio VIIII Hispana', *Ancient Warfare* 4.5 (2010), 48–53

Cichorius, C., *Die Reliefs der Traianssäule*, Berlin: 1900

Connolly, P., *The Roman Army*, London: 1975

Connolly, P., *Greece and Rome at War*, third edition, London: 2006

Cowan, R., 'The Clashing of Weapons and Silent Advances in Roman Battles', *Historia* 56 (2007), 114–17

Durry, M., 'Note sur la tenue des centurions (la crista transversa)', *Revue Archeologique* 27 (1928), 303–08

Forni, G., *Il reclutamento delle legioni da Augusto a Diocleziano*, Milano & Roma: 1953

Forni, G., *Esercito e Marina di Roma Antica* (Mavors vol. 5), Stuttgart: 1992

Gilliam, J. F., 'Milites Caligati', *Transactions and Proceedings of the American Philological Association* 77 (1946), 183–91. Reprinted in Gilliam, *Roman Army Papers* (Mavors vol. 2), Amsterdam: 1986, 43–51

Goldsworthy, A. K., *The Roman Army at War, 100 BC–AD 200*, Oxford: 1996

IMS = *Inscriptions de la Mésie Supérieure*

IRL = Cowan, R., *Imperial Roman Legionary* (Osprey Warrior 72), Oxford: 2003

Isaac, B. H., 'Hierarchy and Command-Structure in the Roman Army' in Isaac, *The Near East Under Roman Rule*, Leiden: 1998, 388–402

MacMullen, R., 'The Legion as a Society', *Historia* 33 (1984), 440–56

Mann, J. C., 'The Raising of New Legions During the Principate', *Hermes* 91 (1963), 175–83

Mann, J. C., 'Roman Legionary Centurial Symbols', *Zeitschrift für Papyrologie und Epigraphik* 115 (1997), 295–98

Mirkovic, M., 'The Roster of the VII Claudia Legion', *Zeitschrift für Papyrologie und Epigraphik* 146 (2004), 211–20

RBT = Cowan, R., *Roman Battle Tactics, 109 BC – AD 313* (Osprey Elite 155), Oxford: 2007

RIB = *Roman Inscriptions of Britain*

RL = Cowan, R., *Roman Legionary, 58 BC – AD 69* (Osprey Warrior 71), Oxford: 2003

Robinson, H. R., *The Armour of Imperial Rome*, London: 1975

Scheidel, W., *Measuring Age, Sex and Death in the Roman Empire*, Ann Arbor: 1996

Speidel, M. A., 'Roman Army Pay Scales', *Journal of Roman Studies* 82 (1992), 87–106

Speidel, M. P., *The Framework of an Imperial Legion*, Caerleon: 1992. A revised version appears in R. J. Brewer (ed.), *The Second Augustan Legion and the Roman Military Machine*, Cardiff: 2002, 125–43

Speidel, M. P, 'Centurial Signs and the Battle Order of the Legions', *Zeitschrift für Papyrologie und Epigraphik* 154 (2005), 286–92

Speidel, M. P, *Emperor Hadrian's Speeches to the African Armies – A New Text*, Mainz: 2006

Stiebel, G., 'Scalping in Roman Palestine – "minime Romanum sacrum"?', *Scripta Classica Israelica* 24 (2005), 151–62

Stoll, O., '»Quod miles vovit …« oder: Der doppelte Ares – Bemerkungen zur Grabstele eines Veteranen aus Alexandria', *Archäologisches Korrespondenzblatt* 35 (2005), 65–76

Sumner, G., *Roman Military Dress*, Stroud: 2009

Tit. Aq. = *Tituli Aquincenses*

Tomlin, R., 'The Missing Lances, or Making the Machine Work' in A. Goldsworthy & I. Haynes (eds), *The Roman Army as a Community*, Portsmouth, Rhode Island: 1999, 127–38

Wheeler, E. L., 'The Legion as Phalanx in the Late Empire, Part II', *Revue des Études Militaires Anciennes 1* (2004), 147–75

# GLOSSARY

| | |
|---|---|
| *Adiutrix* | 'Supportive', legion title |
| *Alaudae* | 'Larks', legion title |
| *Apollinaris* | 'of (the god) Apollo', legion title |
| *aquila* | eagle standard of the legion |
| *aquilifer* | eagle-bearer |
| *armatura* | advanced weapons drill, also title of instructor of the drill |
| *armidoctor* | weapons instructor |
| *Augusta* | 'Augustan', 'of Augustus', legion title |
| *balteus* | military belt, sometimes called *cingulum* |
| *campidoctor* | field instructor |
| *canabae* | civil settlement beside legionary fortress |
| *Castris* | used to denote those 'born in the camp' |
| *Claudia* | legion title derived from the name of the emperor Claudius |
| *centuria* | century, sub-unit of the legion comprising 80 soldiers; six per cohort and 60 per legion |
| centurion (*centurio*) | commander of a century |
| cohort (*cohors*) | formation of six centuries; ten per legion |
| *contubernium* | section of century comprised of eight men who shared a room in barracks or a tent on campaign, but not a tactical unit |
| *cornicularius* | senior clerk |
| *Cyrenaica* | legion title derived from service in the province of Cyrene in North Africa |
| *Deiotariana* | 'of Deiotarus', legion title deriving from Deiotarus of Galatia, its original founder |
| *doctor* | instructor |
| *dolabra* | military pickaxe |
| *duplicarius* | soldier receiving double pay, e.g. *optio*, *signifer* |
| **Equestrian Order** | originally signifying men whose wealth was sufficient to equip them as cavalrymen; equestrians were superior in class to ordinary soldiers (*caligati*) and they could be promoted directly to centurionates (and higher ranks) without prior experience |
| *evocatus* | veteran recalled to service at the request of his commander or emperor to perform a specialist function |
| *Felix* | 'Lucky' or 'Fortunate', legion title |
| *Fidelis* | 'Faithful', legion title |
| *Firma* | 'Steadfast', legion title |
| *Flavia* | 'Flavian', legion title derived from the family name of the emperors Vespasian and Domitian |
| *Fortis* | 'Brave', legion title |
| *Fulminata* | 'Armed with/Bearing Lightning', legion title |
| *Gallica* | 'Gallic' or 'of Gaul', legion title |
| *Gemina* | 'Twin', legion title |
| *Germanica* | 'German', legion title |
| *gladius* | general term for a sword |
| *hasta* | spear |
| *hastatus* | 'spear-armed', centurial title |
| *Hispana* | 'Spanish', legion title |

| | |
|---|---|
| *honesta missio* | honourable discharge |
| *immunis* | soldier given immunity from performing fatigues |
| *Italica* | 'Italian', legion title |
| *iusta legio* | officially recognized legion |
| *labor* | work, toil |
| *lanciarius* | legionary equipped with the *lancea* |
| **legate** (*legatus*) | senatorial commander of the legion |
| *legio* | legion, chief unit of the Roman army, comprised of 60 centuries organized in ten cohorts. Optimum manpower was *c.*5000 (including 120 cavalry), but probably rarely achieved. |
| *librarius* | junior clerk |
| *lorica* | armour |
| *lorica hamata* | mail armour |
| *lorica squamata* | scale armour |
| *lorica segmentata* | articulated armour |
| *Macedonica* | 'Macedonian', legion title |
| *Minervia* | 'of Minerva', legion title deriving from the name of Domitian's favourite goddess |
| *optio* | centurion's deputy; one per century |
| *optio ad spem ordinis* | *optio* marked for promotion to centurion |
| *ordo* | rank or line in battle formation |
| *Pia* | 'Loyal', legion title |
| *pilum* | legionary javelin |
| *pilus* | 'spear/javelin-armed', centurial title |
| *posterior* | 'rear' or 'following', centurial title |
| *praefectus castrorum* | prefect of the camp; equestrian officer, third in command of a legion |
| *praemium* | discharge gratuity |
| *primi ordines* | 'front/first rankers', centurions of first cohort |
| *Primigenia* | 'First born', legion title |
| *primus pilus* | 'first spear or *pilum*', leading centurion of the first cohort and most senior in the legion |
| *princeps* | 'foremost', centurial title |
| *principales* | senior under-officers including the *tesserarius*, *optio* and *signifer* |
| *prior* | 'front', centurial title |
| *pugio* | dagger |
| *Rapax* | 'Grasping', 'Rapacious', legion title |
| *scutum* | curved legionary shield |
| **Senatorial Order** | in Republican times, the ruling class of Rome; remains the upper class in the Empire and provides legions with legates and senior tribunes |
| *sesquiplicarius* | soldier receiving pay-and-a-half, e.g. *tesserarius* |
| *signifer* | standard-bearer, one per century |
| *signum* | standard |
| *spatha* | medium-length or long sword |
| *stipendium* | salary, year of paid service |
| *tesserarius* | officer of the watchword, one per century |
| *tiro* | recruit |
| *Traiana* | 'Trajan's', legion title |